THE MOTOR CAR IN JE

Cover:
Above: the author's Rolls-Royce outside Longueville Manor;
Below: Competitors descending St. Claire Hill into Waterworks Valley at the reliability trials organised by the Jersey Motor Cycle & Light Car Club, February, 1936;

Scene at La Haule, 1936. Beside the road runs the single track of the former railway line from St. Helier to Corbière which was closed by competition from motor transport. Note the 20 mph speed limit sign.

The MOTOR CAR in JERSEY

A short history of a long subject

David Scott Warren

SEAFLOWER BOOKS

Published in 1995 by
SEAFLOWER BOOKS
16 and a half New St. John's Road
St. Helier
Jersey

Seaflower Books is an imprint of Ex Libris Press,
to whom all enquiries and correspondence
should be addressed:

EX LIBRIS PRESS
1 The Shambles
Bradford on Avon
Wiltshire
BA15 1JS

Typeset in 11 point Bookman

Design and typesetting by Ex Libris Press
Cover printed by Shires Press, Trowbridge, Wiltshire
Printed and bound by
Cromwell Press, Broughton Gifford, Wiltshire

© David Scott Warren

ISBN 0 948578 68 8

Contents

Preface by Michael Wilcock	7
A Note on the Illustrations	8
Introduction by the Author	9
EARLY DAYS	7
The Motor Car has arrived – The first Motor Car(s) in Jersey – Dr. Voisin	
MOTORING ORGANISATIONS & MOTOR SPORT	17
The Jersey Motor Association and the Automobile Association – The Royal Automobile Club – The Jersey Motor Cycle & Light Car Club – Road Racing – Hill Climbs – Sand Racing – The Jersey Old Motor Club and the Old Car Interest – Other Motoring Clubs	
MOTORING ADMINISTRATION	45
Motor Tax Department – Motor Traffic Office	
THE OCCUPATION YEARS	61
THE CARS THEMSELVES	71
The Engine – Braking – Car Bodies – Radiators and Mascots – Bumpers – Lighting – Direction Indicators – Windscreen wipers – Heating and Ventilation – Horns	
THE JERSEY MOTOR INDUSTRY	87
Garages – Paragon Garage – Varney's Garage – Colback's Garage – La Motte Garage – St. Helier Garages – Cleveland Garage – Falle's Garage – Roberts' Garage – Advertisements	

ROADS AND FUEL   107
    The Highways – Petrol

THE MOTOR CAR IN JERSEY   115
    Official Cars – Curwood's Traffic Regulations
    Motor Tax – Car Ferries – Parking – Motor
    Museum– Coping with Traffic Growth

Havre Des Pas circa 1930

Preface

To the best of my knowledge this is the first time that the motoring history of Jersey has been recorded.

David Scott Warren's story is quite fascinating and he has unearthed his facts with the thoroughness of a true enthusiast, searching long-forgotten official and company files for every scrap of interesting information about the motor car and the island of Jersey. No mean feat after over 90 years!

Michael Wilcock
Jersey Motor Museum

A Note on the Illustrations

The photographs reproduced in this book are from various sources, as follows:

Pages 6, 89 and 124 – by courtesy of the Jersey Museums Service;
Pages 2, 23 (both), 25, 27, 28, 54 and 114 – by courtesy of the *Jersey Evening Post*;
Pages 29, 33 and 34 – by courtesy of the Jersey Post Office;
Page 116 – by courtesy of Curwood's Garage;
Page 10 – by courtesy of Michael Draper;
Page 39 – by courtesy of Ian D Wright;
Pages 97 (both) and 111 – by courtesy of Michael Willcock;
Pages 38, 41, 42 (both), 43, 73 (both), 75 (both), 77 (both), 78, 79 (upper), 81 (upper), 83 (both) and 85 – by courtesy of Amanda Wright;
All remaining photographs are the author's.

Copyright resides with organisations and individuals as detailed above.

Introduction

This book is not intended for the expert in matters motoring, for he will probably have forgotten more than I shall ever know, but I hope it will provide a little interest to the browser. I have perhaps written it more for my own amusement, and certainly I have derived a great deal of interest from the research that has gone into it. Cars have provided me with a fascination since I had my first pedal car; my Father's Swift Chummy at the time had pretty well the same standard of equipment, except that it did have a windscreen wiper, which, if I remember right, was hand-operated. The pedal car did not have a windscreen.

I have been involved with motor racing for well over forty years, although I have never raced.

Acknowledgement has been made in the text of the enormous help given by the Motor Tax Department (now extinct) and the Motor Traffic Office; this has been welcome. I am grateful, too, to those many people who have been only too willing to give up their time to talk to me, and to give me information. The Jersey Museum Service has helped in many ways, and owns the copyright for several of the pictures; the Postal Department has allowed pictures of stamps. My son has managed to find some gems for me in the course of his own researches into Jersey-French. I have spent many happy hours in the Jersey Motor Museum, and I have been allowed to photograph many of its exhibits. I have also to thank the *Jersey Evening Post* for permission to use several of its photographs.

David Scott Warren
Mont du Ouaisné, Jersey
January 1995

J1 on a De Dion Bouton owned by M Draper Esq. It is doubtful if the rather ornate letters and figures would be permitted today, when the exact size and type are carefully prescribed.

Early Days

The Motor Car has arrived

It came into being only about a century ago; in fact, it was in 1886 that Karl Benz drove a three-wheeled motor car out on test on a cinder track alongside his works in Germany; and it was the following year that he took his second car on the public roads for trial runs. These were done at night, for fear of being banned by the authorities, and the car broke down repeatedly before he had it running successfully.

At much the same time, Gottlieb Daimler, who had previously been working on gas engines, tested a bicycle driven by a motor; the two men had been working independently, but had both developed engines working on a principle described in 1862 by one Herr Otto, that of the four-stroke engine: induction-compression-explosion-exhaust. Put more simply but more long-windedly, an inflammable vapour is introduced into a cylinder, it is then compressed by a piston; a spark sets off an explosion of the vapour which drives the piston the other way, and the used vapour is then discharged. The driving of the piston is harnessed to provide whatever movement is required from the engine.

These two men were by no means the first people to attempt mechanical transport, but they were the first to make it work in practice.

In the very short time since its birth, the motor car has given rise to a change in culture and custom at a speed which must be unprecedented. The ability to travel, first made possible on a practical basis during the last century by the railways, and later by the motor car, is as dramatic a change as that between the Ice

Age and the Iron Age, which took a good deal longer. In our society it is almost impossible to avoid using the motor car or its variants – commercial or public service vehicles – in some way or other. Goods are transported, passengers are carried by road traffic, with great reliability and comfort. Our horizons have been widened by the ability to travel, and especially indeed by the possibility of using our own private transport, and we would not seriously wish to revert to the insularity of our forebears.

The first motor cars were very primitive, consisting of an engine fitted on to what was virtually a horse-drawn vehicle except that it had no horse or means to attach the horse. It was noisy, broke down frequently, and was terrifying to other users of the roads. It gained favour more quickly on the Continent than in Britain, where there was enormous opposition, particularly from the equestrian party; and it only acquired some respectability when the Prince of Wales was taken for a drive by Lord Montagu of Beaulieu, and decided that he liked the beastly thing, somewhere about the turn of the century.

The roads of the day were awful, dust tracks in dry weather and mud in wet. Anything more than a very local journey, which might previously have been done by stage coach, went by rail.

Looking back at the earliest days of the motor car, it had yet to be decided what form it was to take, or even what was to make it work. Electricity rivalled petrol as the source of energy, and indeed electrically-driven cars at one time held the land speed records (the Comte de Chasseloup-Larbat gained it in 1898 and Camille Jenatzy took it off him the following year, at 69.75 mph in *Le Jamais Content*). An electric car was smooth, silent and needed no gear-changing; it was easy to handle, but very limited in its range before the batteries needed recharging, and they were heavy and expensive. Steam, too, provided power which was smooth, silent, and required no gear-changing; but a steam car needed a long time to get an adequate head of steam, unless it had a flash boiler; it was complicated, and had to have a refill of water about every twenty miles.

The author recalls a parade to celebrate fifty years of the motor car in 1946, held in Regent's Park in London; the silence of a steam car of vintage years was only closely rivalled by a very new luxury

Early Days

car. The author Rudyard Kipling had some uncomplimentary remarks to make about his Locomobile steamer, but it was still enough to get him 'hooked' onto the automobile.

Various layouts had to be tried before the front engine driving the rear wheels became generally accepted, and even the number of wheels and their layout had to be decided: one maker tried a lozenge-shaped plan. Latter years have seen a return to the use of various designs, such as front-wheel drive, rear or mid-mounted engines, and four-wheel drive, and most of these have their advantages.

Three-wheelers had a considerable following at one time, strongly aided by lower taxation, provided that the vehicles were below a certain weight, and did not have reverse gears. Four-wheel drive has a dramatic advantage in slippery conditions.

Since its birth the car has become more civilised, more manageable, more versatile and reliable and has, as we know, increased in numbers to a staggering extent world-wide. Jersey has not avoided this explosion, but has embraced its cause wholeheartedly, although it seems to have started late. It has gained a mention in the *Guinness Book of Records* for having the greatest concentration of motor vehicles in the world, and this in an Island not more than ten miles by six, with an estimated six hundred miles of road.

The first Motor Car(s) in Jersey

The *Jersey Express* of 31 July 1899 had an article headed 'A Motor Car for Jersey.' It went on to say:

> A phaeton-built motor car, constructed by the International Motor Company, London, arrived here yesterday for Mr. Peter Falla, Solicitor, of Les Issues, St. John's. This novelty weighs about a hundredweight, and can be driven from three to thirty miles per hour. The car was taken out to Mr. Falla's residence today on a trolley, and we may shortly expect to see the owner travelling on his novel transport.

It had solid tyres, and the Jersey historian, Balleine, tells us it was a 3.5 horse-power Benz, with a dos-a-dos configuration; this means that the driver and front seat passenger faced forwards, while the rear occupants faced backwards. It would seem more likely that the International Motor Company was in fact the supplier, but may have assembled it. An interesting comment is that that the first reference the author found to this new arrival quoted it as having come to the Island on 31 June 1899, which was of course a fundamental improbability. The paper did not get published on 29 or 30 June, let alone June 31.

It must have caused consternation among Mr. Falla's colleagues, and indeed among the whole Island population, but it is unlikely that anyone foresaw the future. It was stoned going up Mont Mado, and became known as *La Machine du Diable*. The quarry at Mont Mado was in production at that time, and the neighbourhood must have been pretty rough. Running the car proved difficult, as there was no petrol supply in the Island, and so this had to be specially brought in, on the ketch *Mizpah*. Handling this dangerous stuff so frightened the stevedoring force that Mr. Falla had to send his man down to collect it from the docks. An interesting vignette is that the car never went out on Sundays, Mr. Falla travelling to Church on his tricycle. It never went out in bad weather, either.

Mr. Falla's man, Barrett, was interested in things mechanical. One day Mr. Falla could not start the car, so he left for Town in his trap. Barrett managed to start it; he caught up with the trap, but was then unable to stop, and sailed past the owner and his son.

The car was finally broken up by Mr. Percy Hunt, at his marine store in Commercial Street. If it were in existence today, it would, of course, be priceless, especially with such provenance. It is understood that until recently a wheel did exist, but this too has now disappeared. The *Evening Post* in 1971 said that the car had arrived seventy-three years earlier, so the arithmetic does not quite add up.

The German maker Benz provided another first for Jersey. A car was built under licence by Grandins', on the Esplanade, a shipbuilding company, possibly from parts and/or drawings supplied by Benz; this, however, may or may not be so, because Imperial measurements were used, while Benz themselves would have used metric. This car, too, has also been described as the first car in

Early Days

Jersey. It was not unusual at the time for the manufacturer either to supply engines and parts to other makers or assemblers, or for other firms to build under licence. The car left the Island for many years, but has now returned, and has been allocated the registration number J0 (zero) by an imaginative Motor Tax Department. It has been displayed at the Annual Dinner of the Jersey Old Motor Club, where it took pride of place. Benz had, of course, produced the world's first viable motor car about fifteen years before this.

J 0, photographed in 1994 (T Bootham).

The conflict between different motive powers has been mentioned. It is not known how many electrically-driven cars there were in Jersey, but there certainly were some.

Dr. Voisin

In 1905 one Dr. Voisin read a paper to the Jersey Medical Society comparing the virtues of a car with those of a horse. This was printed and published by Bigwoods'. He described graphically the difficulties posed to a Jersey doctor by a night call in those days, especially out to the country, for a neighbour of the patient, or one of the family, would have to make his way to the Doctor's residence, preferably with a horse-drawn vehicle, take him to the patient, wait, and then take him back home. It was not unknown for the friend or relation to get tired of waiting, in which case the Doctor would have to find his own way home.

Dr. Voisin totted up the cost to a young practitioner of keeping a horse, with all its extras, compared to that of a car, and found there was very little difference; he then went on to compare the costs to a more established doctor, with three horses, over a year. His figures are interesting, but should, of course, be read with the contemporary value of money taken into account. The outlay for a horse was £100, three horses £300; keep for one year was £120 and £275 respectively. The outlay on a car was £303.5s.11d. (made up by the cost of the car £175, plus carriage from London, and extras, such as lamps). Running costs worked out, on the basis of 10,000 miles at five and a half pence (old money) per mile, to be £154.7s.6d., which included insurance £5.10s., petrol £30.15s, repairs £21.9s.9d., oil, carbide, etc., £9.7s.6d., tyres £30.3s.4d., and cleaner £48.5s. He also compared the noise of the two methods of transport, in favour of the car, which he found reliable. This is interesting today, when we think of cars of that era as being noisy and unreliable. One is reminded, too, of the custom of putting down straw on the road outside a house where there was sickness, to deaden the awful noise of the horses' hooves or iron-shod wheels on hard surfaces. On the question of understanding the 'mechanicals', the good Doctor considered that any member of his profession should have sufficient intelligence to manage.

The Doctor did consider that horses were more convenient for town work, but that elsewhere the car was far more so. He thought that the established Doctor would probably require two cars.

Motoring Organisations & Motor Sport

The Jersey Motor Association and the Automobile Association

The Jersey Motor Association was founded in 1908, 'to help the Jersey motorist.' It published a list of rules of the road, such as 'keep to the left', and how to manage at cross-roads, and so on. Some of these basic rules of the road could perhaps be observed with advantage today, with improvement to safety and traffic flow, and general road behaviour, plus that indefinable thing, the 'courtesy of the road.' The Association had a couple of patrolmen, and its own car badge, which is now very rare.

The Automobile Association was founded in Britain in 1905, also to help the motorist, who was the victim of a persecution by the various authorities, especially on the subject of speed: this refers, of course, to the British mainland. The restrictive 12 mph speed limit law had been rescinded years before that date, but a 20 mph law remained. Speed traps abounded in Britain, and the technique for timing vehicles over a measured distance was highly unscientific and totally inaccurate. One of the duties of the AA patrolman was to warn members of the presence of the trap, but this immediately became illegal, the patrolman being deemed guilty of obstructing the police; so he was instructed simply not to salute a member who was at risk of getting caught in a speed trap,

Overleaf: First few pages of handbook published by The Jersey Motor Association.

PREFACE

ALTHOUGH Jersey is a small Island, being approximately 12 by 7 miles, the actual road surface measures about 486 miles. Apart from the main thoroughfares, many of the roads are narrow, but they wind through delightful scenery, thus making motoring in the Island a pleasure as well as a convenience.

The ratio of motor vehicles to the number of inhabitants in Jersey is one of the highest in the world, the number of registered motor vehicles being over 8,350 and the population approximately 50,000.

It is therefore obvious that, in view of the many narrow circuitous lanes and the abnormally large number of motorists in Jersey, an Association whose interests are entirely public spirited is a necessity, and with adequate support from the motoring public its influence could not fail to be widely felt.

The Jersey Motor Association was founded in the year 1908 with the following objects :—

(1) To assist in the promotion of motoring in the Island, the repression of reckless and inconsiderate driving and helping to prevent ill-feeling against Motorists generally.
(2) To help in the furtherance of public safety, and the convenience of all concerned.
(3) To further the convenience and safety of Motorists by reporting on bad and dangerous corners and roads.
(4) To maintain the right and guard the interests of Motorists.

The membership of the Jersey Motor Association is gradually increasing, and in the proportion that the motoring public gives its support the Association is able to utilise the many opportunities of fulfilling the objects for which it was established.

Do's and Don'ts.

DO carry your driving licence.
DO keep to the left of the road.
DO go slow past schools and in populous places.
DO overtake on the right, after seeing that the road in front is clear.
DO give warnings with the right arm when slowing down or turning to the off-side.
DO conform to the lighting and registration regulations.
DO recognise warning signs and speed restriction notices.
DO realise the discomfort of others of dust and mud splashing.
DO assist the police to regulate traffic by responding promptly to their signals.
DO give the recognised signals with the right arm.
DO answer audible warnings given by drivers of vehicles about to emerge on to a main road from corners and at cross roads.
DO stop when signalled to do so by the J.M.A. Patrol.
DO be considerate to Horse Traffic; stopping and restarting entails a severe strain on Horses.
DON'T abuse the "audible warning of approach."
DON'T drive without a J.M.A. Badge.

Benefits of J.M.A. Membership.

"Get You Home" Scheme.

Members are entitled to a sum not exceeding 10/- in any one year in order to cover the cost of skilled assistance in the event of breakdown on the road occuring to their cars. In order to claim such financial assistance Members should forward full particulars of the breakdown to the Secretary. Members whose subscriptions are in arrear cannot benefit by this assistance.

Patrol Men.

The Association now maintains out of its funds two Patrol Men and with the increasing membership it is hoped that funds will permit of further patrol men being employed. These mens' services have been much appreciated by members and the motoring public particularly in regard to the work they have done in regulating traffic at dangerous corners and crossroads in the various parishes, and in erecting signs, etc.

Port Service.

One of the Association Patrol Men meets all the incoming steamers from England and from France and renders all assistance possible in the unshipping and customs formalities in connection with members cars. A.A. members are entitled to this service also free of cost. Further the patrol man takes charge of members' cars and arranges for their shipment, etc., from Jersey.

Shipping Facilities.

By arrangement with the Railway Companies serving the Island members of the J.M.A. on production of a certificate of membership are granted a rebate on the shipment of cars to France.

In addition cars shipped to England are charged fare and a half for the return journey.

Office Service.

The Office of the Association is at the disposal of all members both for local and for foreign information. The Automobile Association keep us informed daily of the latest news concerning motorists generally. Supplies of literature and Touring Forms are available and every assistance is rendered to members in completing same and obtaining from the A.A. direct, the necessary Documents and sanctions.

Membership Information.

Subscription.

The subscription to the Association is only 10/- (Ten shillings) per annum.

Badges.

A Fee of 5/- is charged to members on joining for the use of the Association's Badge. The Badges are issued on the strict understanding that they are to be only used in the case of private ownership of Cars or Motor Cycles intended for the personal use of members. Badges must be always removed before Cars or Motor Cycles are disposed of or go out of the possession of the members. The Badge remains the property of the Association and must be returned when the membership ceases.

The fee paid for the use thereof is not returnable.

Old Badges can be exchanged for new ones (Chromium Plated) at a fee of 2/-.

Increased Membership.

Members are asked to introduce motoring friends and, by increasing membership, add to the power of the Association.

Resignations.

Any Member wishing to resign shall give notice, in writing, to the Secretary, on or before December 1st in any year; otherwise he shall be liable to pay his Subscription for another year.

Left: Traditional type of AA telephone box still by Trinity Church. Right: Modern AA telephone box at St. Mary. Also to be seen is a 20 mph sign outside St. Mary's Elementary School.

but to salute at all other times. Drivers were advised in the Association handbook to stop and ask why they were not saluted, which, of course, had the effect of stopping any headlong rush. The AA has functioned from the Esplanade since then, providing many services to its members, and, indeed, to the motoring public, with its road signs, roadside telephones, roadside assistance to members, help with foreign touring, and route plans. It also provides a number of publications, such as maps and guide books. Insurance services are an important function.

Motoring Organisations & Motor Sport

The Royal Automobile Club

The Automobile Club, later to be the Royal Automobile Club, had a lower profile in Jersey, but became the governing body of motor sport in the British Isles. This section has now been hived off, and is a separate concern. The Club's original aims were, of course, much the same as those of the AA, namely to help the motorist; and it gave a further service, a Get-You-Home facility, in the event of a breakdown by the roadside. On the one occasion that the author tried to avail himself of this facility, he was refused help since, although his ex-War Department Austin 8 had died near the end of a long journey (for those far-off days; it had been over a hundred miles, and petrol was still rationed in Britain, shortly after the War) within a mile of home, late in the day. It was towed home, and so was no longer on the roadside. He had therefore to pay for a tow to the garage, and then the repair to the damage caused by the gudgeon pin coming out of the small end, which cost all of £9. The service operated on the roadside, and not from a private property. It must be added that this was not in Jersey, and was nearly fifty years ago, and the anecdote is not meant to detract from a most valuable service. The RAC still maintains the service in the Island, and also has an appointed repair agent.

The Jersey Motor Cycle and Light Car Club

The Jersey Motor Club was founded in 1920, with the sole object of promoting motor sport, and the first event to be held was a reliability trial. This was followed by a hill climb at Bouley Bay, and speed competitions on the sands. Various venues for these events have been used since then, and, while sand racing was at one time quite popular on the mainland, it remains only in the Channel Islands. In 1933 a sister club, the Motor Cycle Club, found itself lacking entries for its event, and so a joint meeting was organised with sports car owners, and the ensemble became known as the Jersey Motor Cycle and Light Car Club, whose object remains that of promoting motor sport in the Island. This is done under the auspices of the Royal Automobile Club (Motor Sport), which, as has been mentioned, is the governing body of Motor sport in the British Isles.

Road Racing

Motoring was, of course, in abeyance during the Occupation years, but the Club was reformed in 1944, and added an international road race to its repertoire. The last of these was held in 1952, on a circuit of Victoria Avenue to Bel Royal, the Inner Road to West Park, and round again. It drew famous names in motor racing, such as Prince Bira, Cowell (who was famous for other reasons as well), and many others. Motor racing is, of course, inherently dangerous, and stringent precautions are carried out to minimise the risks; but an horrendous accident took place in 1949; a police sergeant, the Course Medical Officer, and the driver were killed when a Bugatti driven by K W Bear left the road.

The last road race in 1952 was won by I M M Stewart at an average speed of 87.82 mph, in a Jaguar, with Ken Wharton second in a Frazer-Nash, and George Abecassis third. Twenty-nine cars started and twenty-six finished. The 'customary' ball was held that evening at West Park Pavilion, and it was reported that ten thousand tickets were sold for it. Before the race, on 13 March, an act by the Tourism Committee, requesting a guarantee of £2,000 for the holding of a production car race, was lodged au Greffe; and a last moment decision was taken by the Public Works Committee to have the traffic island at West Park removed, as, otherwise, the RAC would not have allowed the race to take place.

Above: In the pits – Jersey entrant Frank Le Gallais' car, J10933
Below: Thirty cars get away for the Final.

Hill Climbs

The Club has an excellent safety record, and serious accidents are, fortunately, rare; but fatalities have occurred at the Hill Climb at Bouley Bay, and at sand racing on the beaches. At one such, on 22 July 1927, a motor cyclist, Clarence John Garnier, was killed on the sand at Millbrook. The Club had not at that time obtained permission to close off a section of the beach, apparently because no one quite knew who should be responsible for giving permission for so doing: possibly it had not occurred to anyone that it was necessary to do this. The Constable of St. Lawrence was severely censured by the Bailiff, Sir William Venables Vernon, who pointed out that he, the Senior Magistrate, was the only person who could have given authority to close the beach; it was otherwise specifically required by law to be open for navigational purposes, the reasonable use of fishermen, and the enjoyment of the public. The Club officials also were in trouble over having broken the law.

There was no First Aid equipment on the spot and no Doctor present. Dr. Mortimer Evans was called, but the casualty died on his way to the Hospital. There was a letter to the Editor of the newspaper the same day as the report of the accident, from a Club official who complained about the numbers of the public who had wandered over the set-out course.

Hill climbs are still held regularly at Bouley Bay. There are two or three a year for the Club members themselves; but the event is also on the National calendar, and once a year top competitors come from the UK, together with a large contingent of RAC (Motor Sport) officials. This event used also to be on the international calendar; at the last one, on 21 July 1955, Ken Wharton was the winner in 55.4 seconds, for the second year running, with Frank Le Gallais second and Dennis Poore third. The fastest times today are in the region of forty seconds – which is fast.

The course runs from outside the Water's Edge Hotel to a line just short of the top of the hill. It is a set length of 1,089 yards, so records can be kept. Competitors' pits are at the bottom of the hill, and along the quay, inevitably overcrowded. The course itself winds, with several sharp and two hairpin bends, and short straights. Part is through woods, and here the surface may be damp, catching out competitors. As in sand racing, there are classes for motor cycles and cars, both racing and 'touring'.

Sand Racing

Sand Racing is a favourite sport of the JMC & LCC. It takes place on either St. Ouen's Beach or, less commonly, Millbrook Beach, these being officially closed off from the public. The tide has to be low, and the course has to be freshly marked out for each occasion, avoiding any patches of soft sand; this means that there cannot be any question of records. Onlookers are able to watch from the beach outside the circuit, or from the sea wall. There are races for cars, both 'production' (highly modified) and racing, and for motor cycles, and competition is keen; some are handicap races. The surface of the sand is quickly broken up, especially on bends, and there is no comparison with a tarmac road. Once a year a forty-lap handicap race for cars takes place, and this puts an enormous strain on cars and drivers. It is great fun to watch.

Sand Racing at St. Ouen's Bay, April 1938. Front-wheel drive Alvis driven by Briginshaw.

The cars are usually highly modified and special radiators are mounted high, to get out of the way of most of the sand being raised by cars in front. There is also a considerable amount of sea-water sprayed up, adding to problems. Life of most of the cars is pretty short, since both sea-water and sand are highly destructive. Big engines may be put into small chassis, giving an enormous power-to-weight ratio.

Another incident took place at sand racing on St. Ouen's beach many years later, when the front wheel of a racing car dug into the soft sand on a corner, tipping the car over; the driver was catapulted out and killed. Problems arose as to which parish was involved, St. Brelade or St. Peter, in order that the appropriate Centenier could be called, as he had to inform the Bailiff's office before the body could be moved. Urgency was lent as the tide was coming in fast; common sense (that uncommon commodity) did prevail in the end.

On another spectacular occasion in 1966, a racing car left the road at high speed during a Sprint meeting on the Five Mile Drive, sliced through a telegraph pole, and turned upside down while still in the air, dropping the driver out. They both proceeded through the air, one above the other, for some distance before landing. The car came to rest in the front wing of a Rolls-Royce among the officials' cars, and driver's head finished up under the wing behind the front wheel. The driver suffered a broken leg and concussion.

It used to be thought good practice at the sand racing to have course marking posts joined by a rope, until a car swerved off the course one day and went under the rope. This caught the driver under the chin and ejected him from the car. He was lucky not to be garrotted, and the practice of joining the posts was not repeated.

The late Sid Logan was a well-known driver, but his car somersaulted on a bend on April 14 1952, throwing him out; he suffered a fractured skull and other injuries, but survived, practically blind.

Safety is strictly adhered to, but fatal accidents can and have taken place; one such is remembered in the name of Sleeman's Corner on Bouley Hill. The Medical Officer of the day was new to the Island, and did not know the strict local rules; so he instructed the Ambulance men to remove the body without having first notified the Centenier or Bailiff, and had to apologise to the

Viscount later, at the inquest. Following this, the medical officer recommended the use of rollover bars and safety belts, but was told they were not necessary. On another occasion an incident took place when an overseas competitor failed to stop at the end of the course, and went on to hit the barrier closing the venue off from the public road.

Crash on the Five Mile Road, 1968.

The Motor Car in Jersey

Another event in 1952 was described as Jersey's second Concours d'Elegance; but the report goes no further than to say that there was a high standard of entries.

The Diamond Jubilee of the JMC& LCC was celebrated with the issue in 1980 of a special set of postage stamps by the Philatelic Bureau; and 1995 will see the 75th anniversary.

Above: Jersey's second Concours d'Elegance, 1952.

Opposite: Special set of postage stamps issued in 1980 by Jersey Philatelic Bureau.

7p	The early days of motor-cycle racing – three lap event near La Rocco Tower.
9p	The great International Road Race – Jersey's Victoria Avenue Circuit.
13p	Post-war Motor-Cycle scrambling – among the wooded valleys.
15p	Sand Racing with cars in the sixties – Corbière Lighthouse in the distance.
17p	Today's National Hill Climb – high performance cars at Bouley Bay.

The Jersey Old Motor Club and the Old car Interest

The Jersey Old Motor Club was founded on 2 November 1966, and provides for the rapidly-growing interest in old cars – mainly those built prior to the Second World War, but of a type which continued to be built for a few years afterwards. The Club is interested in cars built before the end of 1950; it is appreciated that this is an arbitrary date, but there has to be a cut-off somewhere, and the production of the pre-war type of model had come to an end by then. Regular meetings of the club take place on the third Sunday of every month, with a major outing on Boxing Day, and other meetings arranged by the Committee.

The club has about 120 members, but the number of cars is not known; a record is kept of those that are known, but there are several not on the road, while they undergo repair or restoration. Advertised events put on by the Club draw large numbers of onlookers, and are very photogenic. It is hoped that it will be possible in the future to organise a major annual event on a national or even international level, and bringing in entries from Guernsey as well as, in fact, happened in 1993. The growing interest in old cars is pretty general, and does not apply only to Jersey.

The modern garage looks after cars in current or recent production, scrapping parts which are more than a few years old; so the industry of restoration and maintenance of older cars has to be a separate facet of the business. It is possible to spend an almost unlimited amount on a full restoration, which may take years if the owner is sufficiently patient and wealthy; and total wrecks can be rebuilt if enough incentive is there. There is an example in the National Motor Museum at Beaulieu to show the sort of condition in which a car may be found;

Right: Jersey Old Motor Club badge.

found; it may be not much more than a heap of rust, but it can be used as the basis for complete rebuilding. The chassis of a 30 horse-power Rolls-Royce was found blocking the gap in a hedge in Australia, and was used to rebuild a complete car – at enormous expense – but making it the only surviving 30 horse-power Rolls-Royce car out of about forty-five built. In Jersey the industry is slowly building up, and a great amount of the work is done at home by owners, on a very amateur basis. On the Mainland there is a considerable number of such firms which work to a very high standard; but it is wide open to cowboys, who also exist. Rebuilds of two similar engines in 1969 and 1985 cost £400 and £4,000, which, allowing for money values, were practically identical figures.

Stocks of spare parts come from cars which have been broken up in the past, or, in a few cases, which have been salvaged after being thrown out. Other parts may have to be made, which puts up the cost. One-make car clubs have a valuable part to play in the stocking of parts, and also of technical know-how. Where there was a high production of cars, such as the Austin 7, one can expect a fairly large amount of spares to exist, while the high number of surviving cars is only a small proportion of those made; in the case however of low-production cars, as, for instance, the Morris Major, there is not likely to be many parts. Expensive makes, such as Rolls-Royce, of which not so many were built, were more carefully looked after, often by chauffeurs, so that those which remain are a comparatively large proportion of those produced, and a significant section of the industry is devoted to such single marques.

Opposite:

Commemorative stamp issue for 1989 by the Jersey Philatelic Bureau began a new thematic series 'Vintage Cars' which are owned by local residents. From the wealth of excellent motor vehicles in the Island, the cars depicted are selected for their outstanding popularity, prestige, power, prettiness and/or distinction.

Placed against Jersey backgrounds of their day, the models are:

12p   Talbot Type 4CT 16HP Tourer in a vraicing scene, Le Hocq (circa 1912).

16p   De Dion Bouton Type 1-D, at a picnic in the ruins of Grosnez Castle (circa 1920).

22p   Austin 7 'Chummy' at Jersey's last working brick kiln, Mont a l'Abbé (circa 1920).

29p   Ford Model T during the digging of the Jersey Royal Potato crop (circa 1926).

31p   Bentley 8 Litre outside the Guard House of Government House (circa 1926).

34p   Cadillac 452-V16 Fleetwood Sports Phaeton outside St. Ouen's Manor Lodge (circa 1931).

1912 Talbot Type 4CT 16hp Tourer
JERSEY
12

1920 De Dion Bouton Type I-D
16
JERSEY

1926 Austin Seven 7hp 'Chummy'
J1056
JERSEY
22

1926 Ford Model T
29
JERSEY

1930 Bentley 8 Litre
J2603
JERSEY
31

1931 Cadillac #52 V16 Fleetwood Sports Phaeton
34
JERSEY

1925 Morris Cowley "Bullnose"
JERSEY
16p

1932 Rolls Royce 20/25
JERSEY
22p

1924 Chenard & Walcker T5
JERSEY
28p

1932 Packard 900 Series Light Eight
JERSEY
33p

1927 Lanchester 21
JERSEY
39p

1918 Buick 30 Roadster
JERSEY
50p

Opposite:

A second set of stamps issued in 1992 by Jersey Philatelic Bureau depicting Vintage Cars which are registered in Jersey and owned by local residents.

Each model is placed against a Jersey background of its day:

16p   1925 Morris Cowley 'Bullnose' at L'Etacquerel.

22p   1932 Rolls Royce 20/25 in The Parade.

28p   1924 Chenard & Walcker T5 near St. Catherine's.

33p   1932 Packard 900 Series Light Eight, N.E. Coast.

39p   1927 Lanchester 21, The Old Rectory, St. Saviour.

50p   1913 Buick 30 Roadster, Broad Street.

Case History: 1937 Talbot BD75

It is interesting to look into the history of older cars, and an example may be described. The car in question is a Talbot BD 75, which has a 2.276 litre, 17.9 horse-power engine; chassis number 2888 and engine number 393. The chassis and engine were assembled at the Talbot works in London, and went to the coach-builders, the Carlton Carriage Company, on 13 April 1937. It returned with a drop-head coupe body on 2 June 1937, and was dispatched to the Thornton Engineering Co. Ltd. in Bradford on 12 June for sale. It was given to a Mr. Ronald Hare in Wetherby, as its second owner when it was three months old, for his twenty-first birthday. He owned it until after the War, when a neighbour persuaded him to part with it, but it only moved up the road, and continued to be looked after by the same engineer. After some years Mr. Hare bought it back, but he or his son sold it to a dealer around 1980. At some time during the War years it is reputed to have had the hood peppered with gunshot in the shooting field, but there was no evidence of this when the car came to Jersey; the hood however did appear to have been replaced at some time, and not very well done. It has been in the Island since 1981, and has been the subject of fairly considerable restoration in that time, although piecemeal, but it has never been laid up for a complete strip and rebuild. It was painted a very uninspired grey and black when it came, and has been resprayed blue. It is by no means immaculate or in concours condition, but is very usable. The mileage is believed to be in the region of 95,000 miles.

While driving along the Route de Noirmont one fine day, the car hit a pothole which had been left by some of the diggers-up-of-roads. The rear-hinged nearside door flew open, and hit the wall. As the car was moving forwards, this did a lot of damage to the door and door pillar, which took 364 days to repair, and no damage to the wall. The bodywork is wood-framed, with aluminium skin to the doors, so it required both carpenter and metal-worker to put it right; fortunately, some of the pot of blue cellulose used in the spraying of the car was still available, so an accurate colour-match was achieved with a minimum of trouble. The car remains in regular use, not doing a very high mileage.

Motoring Organisations & Motor Sport

The author's Talbot BD 75, subject of the Case History opposite.

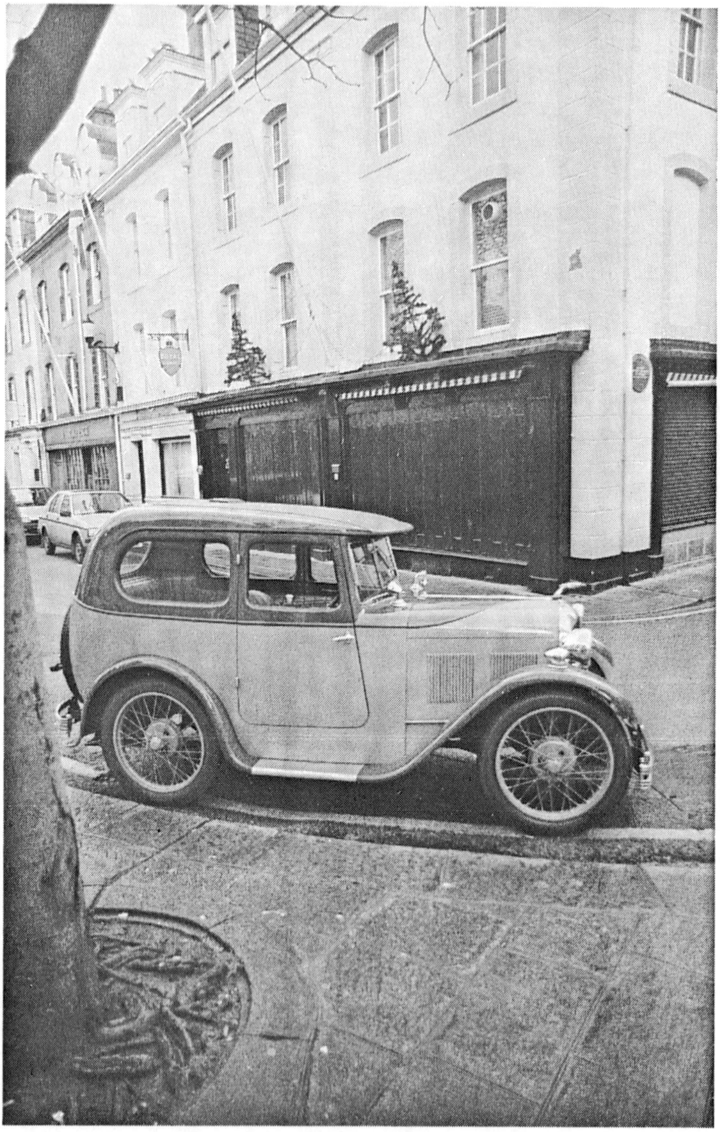

Above: 1938 Talbot 10 (I D Wright).
Opposite: Austin 7 Swallow. Bodywork built by Swallow Sidecars, which evolved into Jaguar Cars (A Tate).

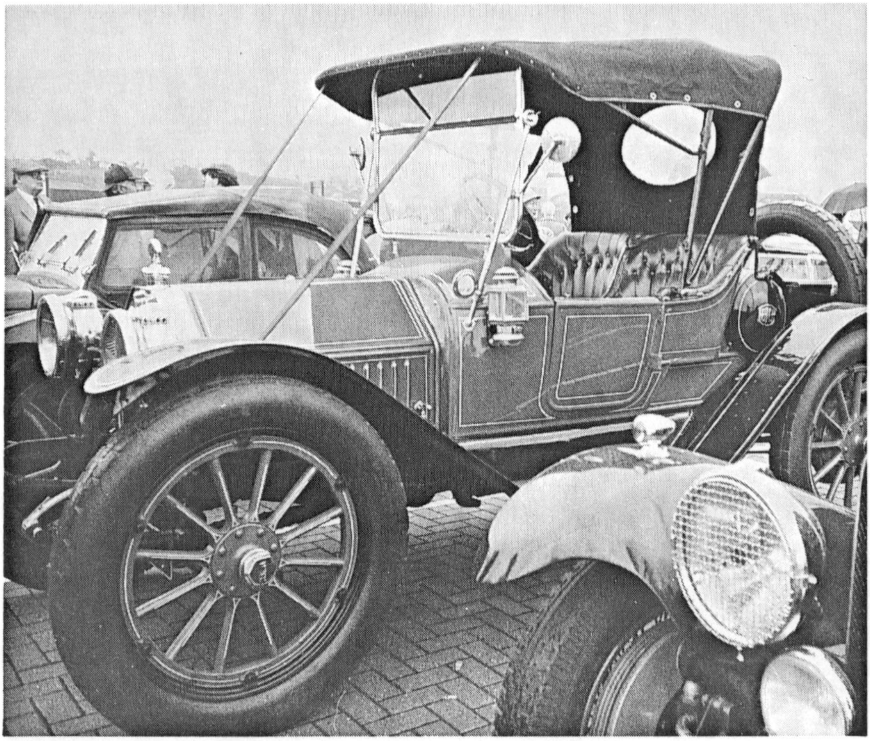

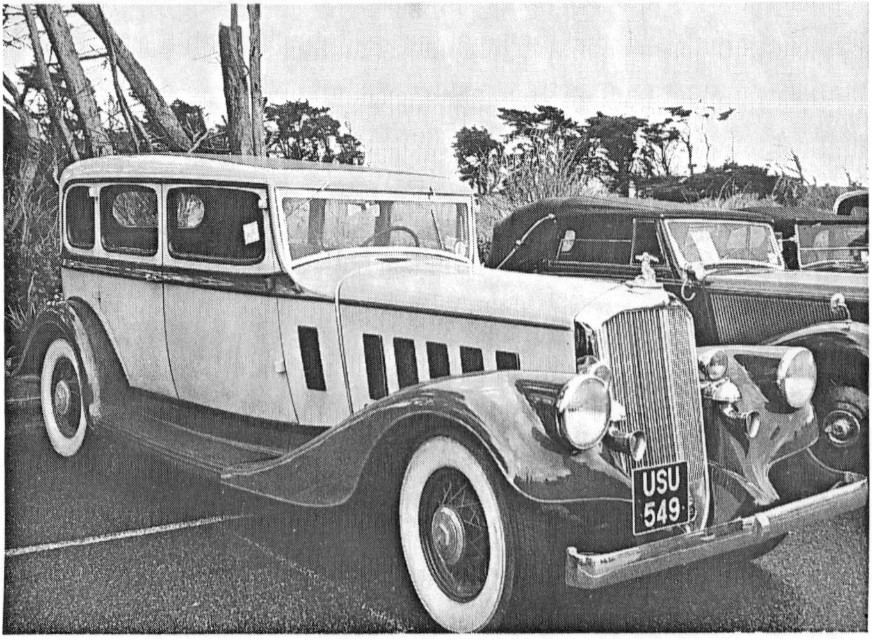
USU
549

Above and opposite above: 1913 Buick with hood up and down (G Bisson). There are two 'with-it' types of number plate, to compare with personalised plates in the UK; either a low number, or, as here, showing the year of manufacture of the car.

Opposite below: Pierce-Arrow brought into the Island by Le Riche Investments Ltd.

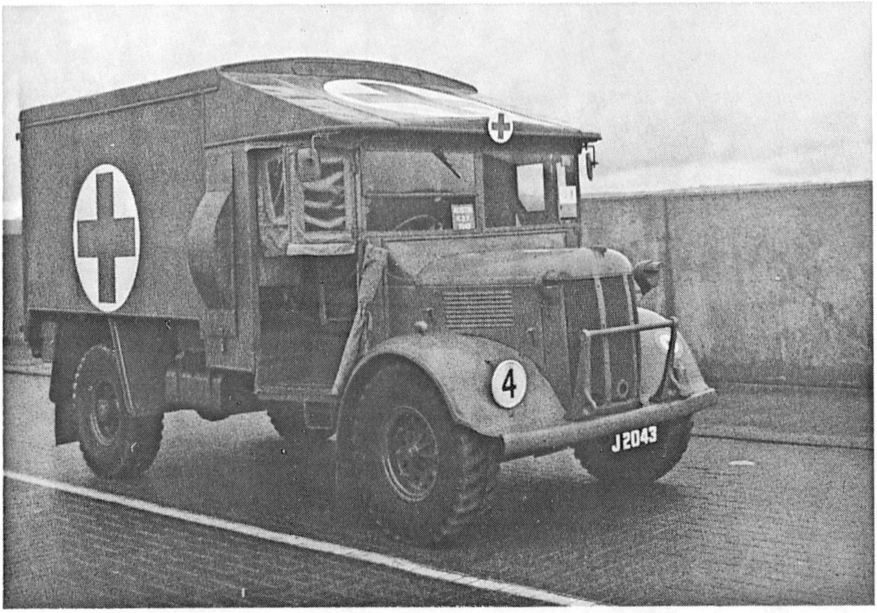
4
J2043

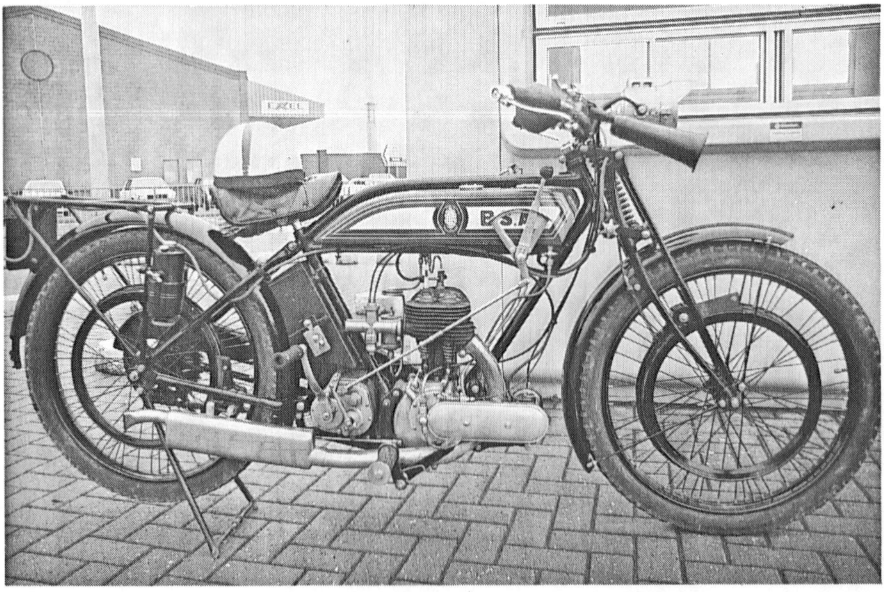

Above: Author's Talbot BD75. Poor side visibility can be noted; also elegant wind-tone horns.
Opposite above: Austin K2 Ambulance, 1942 (G Stye). Used after the War at Guernsey Airport.
Opposite below: BSA Motorcycle, 1925 (R A Rault).

Other Motoring Clubs

There exists at the present time a loose organisation (it would probably prefer to call itself a non-organisation) known as the Jersey Transport Enthusiasts, with regular gets-together. This is open to anyone interested in any form of transport in the Island, and its meetings are attended by a fair number of motor cycles, and cars which are more or less evenly balanced between old and modern. At the time of writing, these regular meetings are held on the first Sunday of every month, at the Harvest Barn.

The term 'classic' car has yet to be defined, but is usually taken to mean a post-war car, no longer in production. This gives a dignity to some which are most certainly not classics, but it underlines the impossibility of any accurate definition in this sort of field. A Classic Car Club was formed in 1992 with an even looser definition of 'Classic' – simply a car which one wanted or enjoyed, whatever it might be, the definition just being that of the owner. This club meets regularly at the Old Portelet Inn, the members showing great enthusiasm.

This does leave a gap in Club interest in the history of motoring heritage, from 1950 onwards, and it seems important that it should be filled. There is a large number of cars or marques which most certainly deserve the name 'Classic' and merit great interest and preservation.

There is a number of one-make clubs, which specialise. These include, among others, the MG Car Club, and the Rolls-Royce Enthusiasts Club. They share the common interest between the members, and can provide help with problems, such as technical queries or spare parts. It is not easy to gather enough of any one make in the Island to create an active one-make club.

There is a branch of the Royal Society for the Prevention of Accidents (ROSPA) which undertakes advanced driving instruction and tests. Regular meetings of this organisation take place at the Motor Traffic Office on the first Sunday of the month.

Motoring Administration

Motor Tax Department

The Motor Tax Department came into being on 1 January 1915, in pursuance of a Loi sur la Voirie of 10 August 1914. This provided for registration and – not surprisingly – taxing of vehicles: all vehicles registered in the Island are under the heading J. It came to its end with the close of 1993, when the annual motor tax was discontinued. The first car to be registered, J 1, was a de Dion Bouton, belonging to Ernest Walker, of Tower Road. J 1 is still on a de Dion Bouton (see illustration on page 10), but this is not the original one, as it was not built until 1920, and was originally registered in Normandy, but was probably brought to Jersey very shortly afterwards. It still has Norman number plates behind the Jersey ones. It was brought into the Island by one Mr. Moncrieff-Simpson, but it is not certain just when this was. It now belongs to Mr. Michael Draper. A recent suggestion that the number might be sold separately from the car was met with the advice that the number remained the property of the States Department, which would take it back if this happened; effectively, it was not saleable separately. In fact, it has recently become possible to retain a J number, transferring it from car to car, for the sum of £50 for each car, while in the past it was only possible to retain a number if the car to which it was attached was leaving the Island, and the receiving car was unregistered in Jersey.

Pedal cycles also had to be registered, have a J number, and pay tax, and quite a large proportion of the first year's registrations was of bicycles.

Taxation rates on motor vehicles were:

Motor cycles with two wheels, or each
  auto wheel attached to a bicycle: £1
Motor cycle with three wheels or sidecar: £1.10s.
Cycle car (not exceeding 800 pounds): £2
Car up to 20 h.p. or 2 tons: £3
Car over 20 horse-power.: £3 plus 5s. per h.p.
Car over 2 tons: Excess of £1 per half ton or part thereof.

These rates remained until after the War, and from 1950 they were:

Motorcycle or three-wheeler: £2
Cycle car up to 800 ponds: £3
Car up to 20 horse-power: £5
Car over 20 horse-power: £5 plus 7s.6d. per h.p.
Car over 2 tons: £1 per extra half ton or part thereof.
Tractor for agricultural purposes only: 5s.

While these figures seem very low, the contemporary value of money should once again be considered; the tax was relatively a good deal higher than it was as the annual motor tax came to its end with 1993.

At the end of 1915, 543 vehicles had been registered; in 1916 the number had increased to 644, and in 1917 to 688, and the J numbers matched.

At the outbreak of war, in 1939, the J numbers had reached 11944, and at the end of 1945, 11960. Many cars disappeared during the war, many were commandeered and removed by the Germans; but with the onset of peace the Channel Islands became part of the export market as far as the UK was concerned, and so, while there was a severe shortage of new cars in Britain, they were available on the local market, to counter the severe shortage of any cars.

In 1980 the J numbers were up to 68900, and about the same in 1983. As vehicles were withdrawn from use, the J numbers were re-used, but it is uncertain when this practice started. Large quantities of them became available when, for instance, organisations such as the Post Office were mechanised, and their many traditional bicycles were scrapped, and again when the bicycle tax was rescinded altogether. There was an explosion of registrations in the eighties, when hire companies expanded, but, in fact, they did not use all the numbers allocated to them, so it is impossible to draw conclusions about the numbers of vehicles on the road from the J numbers issued. The lists featured on pages 48-51 show the annual limits of J numbers issued, and also the numbers registered, and a breakdown of what those vehicles were (by courtesy of the old Motor Tax Department).

Log, or registration books became compulsory about 1964; prior to that, they were required only for overseas travel. Today the traditional log book is in the process of change to a rather nasty, but just as efficient, paper document, and owners of old cars, who want to keep their traditional books, are watching very carefully. The new log books do not show anything of the car's history, and they describe the car under very limited headings; no provision is made, for instance, for the traditional 'open tourer.' The old log book can be kept under certain circumstances.

In latter years it has become very much a cult thing to have a low J number, but it is obviously not possible to have 'personalised' numbers, as in the UK.

In 1966 the basis of taxation was altered to that of length, but it was abolished altogether at the end of 1993, the revenue to be maintained by increasing the tax on petrol. Prior to this, the maximum tax by length was £60 for a car over 16 feet in length. Petrol is much cheaper here than in the UK, if not than throughout Europe, and will, hopefully, remain so; but consumption is much higher, owing to the number of short runs. It is now necessary to carry a current insurance disc on the windscreen in place of the old tax disc, but it was too much to hope that these would be designed to fit in the old round tax disc holders. The new system is in operation in a number of communities already.

Number of Vehicles licensed and taxed as at 31 December

Year	Moped	Motor cycle	Motor Car	Taxi	Van
1926		951	2335		
1927		989	2600		
1928		1007	2862		
1929		1050	3230		
1930		1050	3602		
1931		1052	4090		
1932		1045	4695		
1933		1030	5474		
1934		980	6420		
1935		909	7103		
1936		885	7493		
1937		823	7924		
1938		767	8452		
1939		750	8420		
1940					
1941					
1942	Island occupied by German Military Forces
1943					
1944					
1945					
1946		1173	4427		
1947		1431	6080		
1948	136	1503	6704	204	1254
1949	156	1544	6748	155	1357
1950	182	1743	6215	165	1299
1951	205	1874	5906	131	1279
1952	232	1913	6235	125	1340
1953	226	2019	6962	149	1408
1954	258	2018	7813	154	1515
1955	318	2061	8587	150	1600
1956	359	2099	9079	158	1658
1957	897	2034	9847	200	1837
1958	1024	2021	10811	191	1892
1959	1314	2018	12290	205	1994
1960	1629	1867	14065	243	2029

Truck	Bus	Coach	Tractor	Miscellaneous	Total
					3286
					3589
					3869
					4280
					4652
					5146
					5740
					6504
					7400
					8012
					8378
					8747
					9219
					9170
					7389
					944
Island occupied by German Military Forces					736
					632
					557
					4446
2082					7682
2468					9979
2113	75	100	101	12	12202
2149	82	79	736	12	13018
2098	83	83	762	11	12641
2008	88	82	815	15	12403
1967	91	91	861	24	12879
1941	109	102	890	55	13861
1932	100	116	920	60	14886
1921	106	116	975	57	15891
1880	104	138	1012	97	16584
1907	94	148	1080	81	18125
1954	98	158	1121	125	19395
1987	98	157	1196	145	21404
1966	104	176	1269	195	23543

Year	Moped	Motor cycle	Motor Car	Taxi	Van
1961	1887	1703	15684	258	2095
1962	1935	1547	17382	288	2228
1963	1941	1482	18937	250	2255
1964	2115	1342	20813	229	1904
1965	2061	1328	22284	232	2030
1966	2213	1114	24022	266	2018
1967	2098	1251	25650	250	2161
1968	1915	1181	27365	232	2245
1969	1715	1159	29688	238	2402
1970	1775	905	31451	239	2431
1971	1609	992	32572	216	2631
1972	1499	795	34310	127	2551
1973	1408	763	36145	114	2643
1974	1315	852	36920	144	2780
1975	1336	877	38173	132	2906
1976	1538	1337	39006	118	3055
1977	1650	1664	40335	104	3178
1978	1529	2013	42173	97	3354
1979	1338	2622	43655	93	3444
1980	1596	2735	44464	88	3481
1981	1584	2951	43828	91	3395
1982	1633	3191	44593		3495
1983	1532	3392	46717		3502
1984	1446	3342	48646		3696
1985	1342	3258	52613		3803
1986	1288	3056	57175		3973
1987	1283	2826	58424		4227
1988	1075	2933	61214		4483
1989	1038	2891	60747		4679
1990	937	3019	61878		4980
1991	984	2896	59466		5231
1992	997	2807	60396		5333

Truck	Bus	Coach	Tractor	Miscellaneous	Total
1988	98	191	1304	191	25399
2095	90	215	1367	177	27324
2001	109	207	1419	249	28850
1977	94	243	1458	355	30530
2055	79	263	1477	307	32116
1921	80	272	1542	361	33809
1942	103	280	1633	394	35762
1936	97	296	1648	431	37346
1877	99	282	1736	449	39645
1930	106	292	1734	509	41372
1775	71	320	1734	597	42517
1796	74	375	1715	652	43894
1817	74	412	1731	581	45697
1835	110	416	1758	611	46741
1830	142	402	1821	518	48137
1806	58	491	1830	638	49877
1775	65	539	1848	600	51758
1797	58	577	1957	649	54204
1857	59	694	1982	634	56378
1725	63	614	1954	689	57409
1797	68	621	1971	594	56900
1709	66	609	1989	781	58066
1745	59	629	2040	699	60315
1774	60	654	2100	660	62378
1804	65	655	2076	748	66364
1777	62	639	2080	656	70706
1878	54	655	2121	766	72234
1932	66	663	2122	740	75228
1882	65	667	2153	866	74988
1908	46	670	2276	929	76634
2047	65	662	2209	805	74365
2002	74	620	2279	712	75220

Motor Traffic Office

This would appear to have come into being on Boxing Day, 1851, when an Order in Council was made at Sandringham, providing for the policing of roads, beaches, and parks. This permitted the States of Jersey to act by regulation, and so, arguably, all the laws which have been passed since then on that subject might be considered superfluous. One Louis Robert was fined five shillings on July 21 1902, 'for furious cycle riding', and this would have come under such regulation. Nevertheless, in 1935 a law was passed, La Loi sur la Circulation d'Automobiles, bringing into actual being the Motor Traffic Office, whose function originally was to control public service vehicles, such as buses and taxis. A further law, the Road Traffic (Jersey) law, was passed in 1956, to tighten up on road traffic in general. It came under the control of the Defence Committee, but it is not known just when this took place.

Effectively, prior to 1935, there had been little or no formal control of public service vehicles, the Constables exercising such control as there was. An order of 1899 had required that the Constables have registers of passenger vehicles, and that they (the vehicles, not the Constables) have numbers prominently displayed. Later, as buses became more common, and as most of them were registered in St. Helier, the Constable of this parish kept a qualified mechanic to ensure the standard of the buses.

The first Chief Officer of the Motor Traffic Office was a Mr. La Cloche, although there seems to have been no formal appointment; the annual salary was £350. Junior Traffic Officers, who became Chief Officers in later years, were Percy Thomas Amy Macready, Harold Michel, and today Mr. Brian Rondel holds that post. Macready's father, Reginald Amy Macready, a Jerseyman, had been associated with the Hon. C S Rolls, and later with the Rolls-Royce Motor Company; he appears as Driver-Mechanician Macready on Rolls' visit to America in 1906, and afterwards on some of Rolls-Royce' record-breaking exploits. Earlier, Macready had worked at Barnes' Garage, and had chauffeured on some continental tours, so it seems likely that this is where he had met Rolls.

The first records of driving tests appear in 1936; compulsory

Motoring Administration

third party insurance did not come into effect until 1948. The cost of a driving test after the war was 7s.6d., and the required competence does not seem to have been very high by any standard. Driving lessons were given, if indeed any were given, as often by a friend or relation as by a driving instructor; the dealer supplying the car might well give a lesson or two. The actual issue of licences to drive has remained a function of the parish authorities, until 1994, when it became centralised at La Colette.

The Motor Vehicle (Construction and Use) Order came into effect in 1956, to control the roadworthiness of vehicles. The MOT test is not applicable to Jersey, but unroadworthy vehicles can be taken off the road with immediate effect. The Motor Vehicle (International Circulation) order was introduced in 1933, although it was not implemented until 1958; this in turn was the result of a Geneva Convention of 1931, and had the effect of road-testing vehicles prior to foreign tours. This order has still not been rescinded, but has not in fact been enforced for many years. The author remembers the test being carried out; he used to take his car in for testing himself at first, but tests, such as that on the braking, demanded so much rubber being left on the road that he found it kinder to himself, if not to the car, if his garage agents did this for him.

The principal function of the Motor Traffic Committee remained that of the control of public service vehicles in the days up to the 1939 War; buses and taxis were authorised, licences granted, licences withdrawn, drivers suspended and reinstated. During the war it was the line of communication between the Occupying Authority and the Island's Transport Authority; this is dealt with in another section, and copies of a number of communications between the German authorities and the local administration will be attached, also by courtesy of the Motor Traffic Office.

A few highlights show up. On 3 February 1936 the committee authorised its Inspector to purchase a second-hand car for a price not exceeding £100, which would be enough to buy a perfectly good second-hand car – or even a new one. Six weeks later, the Inspector was to recommend two men for the post of Traffic Officer at £3 per week; this is where Messrs. Macready and Michel appeared. On 24 December it minuted that they were 'to be released from duty on

Christmas Day, and the duties to be curtailed on Boxing Day.' It decided quite early in its career that, in char-a-bancs, three children should count as two adults.

Standards of vehicles were maintained, and timetables drawn up. On 30 April 1936 it was decided that 'no new licences are to be issued for open cars on cab ranks' (their language). Prior to this open cars could be used as taxis.

Jersey Traffic Inspectors in 1936.
From left to right: Mr H C Michel, Mr G F La Cloche (Chief Inspector) and Mr P T A Macready.

On 12 July 1939 (only just before the outbreak of War) the Committee considered a letter from the Jersey Motor Association over the issue of International Driving Permits, and decided that that application could not be granted, although there was nothing to say what the matter was about. This seems to be the first time that the Committee had dealt with affairs concerning the private motorist.

On 8 December 1939, the Inspector, Mr. La Cloche, was ill, and Tom Macready was appointed Inspecteur Agissant.

It was also noted that the other Traffic Officer had been absent from duty without permission, and he was severely reprimanded, suspended for three weeks without pay, and reduced to the position of Third Traffic Officer (there does not appear effectively to have been any second Traffic Officer at that time – Gilbert and Sullivan beware!) La Cloche resigned the following February, on account of ill-health, and Macready was appointed in his place on 1 April, at £300 per annum, with augmentations of £12.10s. up to £350 (their language).

A Mrs. Sheila Picot, who died aged about 103 years, is understood to have been the first woman to ride a motor cycle combination. When she applied to the Constable of Trinity for a licence for this in 1910 he asked if she could drive it; and she volunteered that, if he cared to ride on the pillion, she would demonstrate. We are not told if he accepted.

One serious accident took place on 19 August 1934, when a motorist knocked down and killed a pedestrian on the Weighbridge. He was charged with 'driving at a dangerous speed, driving at a danger to the public, by want of skill, and by imprudence, collided with ... , inflicting injuries which caused death.' It happened at night, when apparently the pedestrian started to cross the road, suddenly hesitated, and then turned back. The driver was described in Court as skilled, and he was driving a Buick said to be in good order as regards lights and brakes. Nevertheless he was committed to twelve months hard labour. An appeal was heard some twenty months later, which was a *cause célèbre*, with well-known names on both sides; among other things it was said that speed *per se* was not evidence of negligence. The appeal was lost.

Some major post-war developments have been in the fields of drinking and driving (Article 16 of the 1956 Jersey law).

In the older days one had to be pretty unfit to be deemed unfit to drive, but matters have been tightened over the years, and are now very strict. Decisions used to rely on the examining doctor's opinion, and then alcohol concentrations in the urine and blood came to be measured. At first these were not officially recognised, but were only supportive, or otherwise, to the physical examination, although the Police Court did note them. The Police Surgeon

The Motor Car in Jersey

in the early sixties prepared a report for the Police on the question of relying on the blood and urine concentrations of alcohol, at the request of the Chief Officer, E H Le Brocq, and which he recommended. Today the Breathalyser is used. It has to be remembered that different people may react to a given amount of alcohol in different degrees; but alcohol is a sedative, and the question must arise as to whether one should drive after any drink. Reactions are slowed by a measurable amount after even a small amount of alcohol, and one does not by any means have to be drunk to be unfit to drive.

A story which gave rise to some amusement concerned a doctor who was a disciple of Bacchus. He attended his surgery in Town one day, having, of course, parked his car outside, but afterwards appears to have walked home, a distance of several miles, in an alcoholic haze. The following morning, on finding his garage empty (one just did not leave one's car in the open in those days) he reported its loss to the police. It was not a terribly serious offence at that time.

A 40 mph speed limit was introduced in about 1960. The *Evening Post* had been campaigning for some time for a limit, and action was taken after an horrendous weekend, in which three pedestrians were killed on the roads in separate accidents, the pedestrian in each case being in the middle of the road. Today there is an Island-wide speed limit of 40 mph, with lower limits in some built-up areas.

A crop of traffic lights arrived in the 1950's. Prior to that, the only one had been outside an aircraft hangar in St. Peter, which was on the other side of the road from the Airport itself. Shortly after this, two local dignitaries, professional colleagues, were together in a car being driven by one of them, an ex-Senator, who shot over the red light, to the horror of the other. The driver's reply to his companion's strongly-worded comment was, 'It's all right, A., they are only for the visitors.'

There had been a Road Traffic (Jersey) Law in 1935, which was amended in 1956. This required that every road accident had to be reported to the Police, States or honorary. At that time the States Police had no jurisdiction outside St. Helier, and were frequently very unwelcome in some of the country parishes. This

Motoring Administration

ruling was itself amended to that of requiring only certain categories of accident to be reported:

> Damage to an unattended vehicle.
> Damage to a third party's wall or gate.
> Injury to person or animal (except cat or bird).
> Only one's own car involved.

The Police Force (Jersey) Law empowered the States Police to act within the territorial limits of the Bailiwick.

The law with regard to the construction and use of vehicles which came into force in 1956, looked to the roadworthiness and safety of and to vehicles and other road users. This required, among other things, that loads should be properly secured, and that the vehicles themselves should be safe. It has been mentioned that an unsafe car can be ordered off the road with immediate effect. It also banned flushing toilets in cars, but did allow colour televisions; in all, the general intention was to ensure a satisfactory state of any road user. It did not require crash-testing of vehicles, so that legally some cars may be sold in the Island that are not permitted in most other parts of the British Isles.

Driving Tests

Year	Pass	%	Fail	Total
1936	653	89.4	77	730
1937	1186	94.0	77	1263
1938	1086	91.7	98	1184
1939	841	89.1	102	943
1940				
1941				
1942	951	92.3	79	1030
1943				
1944				
1945				
1946	1221	80.7	291	1512
1947	1152	75.8	367	1519
1948	1181	70.7	488	1669
1949	1014	70.8	418	1432
1950	769	72.0	299	1068
1951	673	71.4	269	942
1952	732	65.5	385	1117
1953	981	68.7	445	1426
1954	953	67.3	462	1415
1955	1123	69.4	495	1618
1956	1172	69.2	521	1693
1957	1062	76.0	332	1394
1958	1578	77.0	474	2052
1959	1638	71.0	667	2305
1960	2161	74.0	758	2919
1961	2988	73.8	1059	4047
1962	3197	74.6	1085	3282
1963	2793	73.5	1006	3799
1964	2736	72.6	1028	3764
1965	2903	74.4	1004	3934
1966	2504	74.0	875	3379
1967	2519	74.0	863	3382
1968	2577	73.0	938	3515
1969	2597	71.0	1060	3657
1970	2736	73.8	969	3705

Year	Pass	%	Fail	Total
1971	2805	76.0	890	3695
1972	2828	81.7	633	3461
1973	2727	78.0	754	3481
1974	2889	79.0	761	3650
1975	2933	77.0	833	3766
1976	3197	74.0	1076	4273
1977	3118	74.5	1063	4181
1978	2920	72.8	1086	4006
1979	3223	75.0	1073	4296
1980	3255	76.3	1033	4288
1981	2634	69.6	1149	3783
1982	2719	71.3	1096	3815
1983	2793	71.9	1105	3898
1984	2800	66.1	1450	4250
1985	2787	66.0	1420	4208
1986	2734	65.8	1427	4161
1987	2677	66.2	1409	4086
1988	2633	66.3	1335	3968
1989	2507	61.1	1599	4106
1990	2659	60.6	1723	4382
1991	3245	63.6	1855	5100
1992	2656	57.4	1944	4600

Vehicles visiting Jersey.

Year	Number
1968	4169
1969	4178
1970	3182
1971	3082
1972	2675
1973	6001 (Introduction of Roll-On-Roll-Off from Weymouth)
1974	10024
1975	9696
1976	11748
1977	16746
1978	30122 (24815 cars; Introduction of RoRo from Portsmouth)
1979	33035 (26639 cars)
1980	32746 (26334 cars)
1981	29525 (23417 cars)
1982	29974 (23425 cars)
1983	32569 (25184 cars)
1984	28519 (21887 cars)
1985	29913 (21478 cars)
1986	34013 (24712 cars)
1987	29334 (19762 cars)
1988	31473 (21295 cars)
1989	40765 (28147 cars)
1990	46103 (29156 cars)
1991	47579 (28435 cars)
1992	46372 (25981 cars)

Trade cars including hire cars

	In	Out
1989	11847	7824
1990	15075	11353
1991	11444	7336
1992	12067	9140

Trade cars include all new cars, second-hand cars and hire cars.
The Trade figures are in addition to the total visiting vehicles.

The Occupation Years

During the Occupation years of 1940-'45 there were, of course, no new cars brought to the Island, at any rate for civilian use, the Occupying Authority commandeering many that were here and paying for some of them on its own valuation. There is, nevertheless, an Austin 10 (1934) still in the Island which belonged to a Doctor Sandberg, who died during the Occupation; it was bought from his estate after the War for £65 by Mr. Barry de la Mare, and it has initials carved on the steering wheel by a child patient. It appears, too, that the Germans preferred new or newish cars, and, anyway, a Doctor's car could be considered essential to civilian life.

A story concerns the owner of a nearly-new lorry, who had to take it for examination and requisitioning. He messed around with the electrics, until it ran so badly that when the German Inspector saw it he told him to take it away. He related this to a friend who did the same thing to his truck. Unfortunately for him, the Inspector said that it was running so badly that it was worth practically nothing, and that was what he would give.

The issue of new J numbers during the War years shows clearly the lack of new vehicles being registered, with an increase of 16; it may be assumed that the Germans brought in some vehicles for their own use.

At the start of the Occupation the Germans took control of stocks of petrol, and ordered all public transport to cease. The civil authority protested at this, and limited services were allowed to restart, using twenty-nine vehicles which consumed about fifteen hundred gallons of fuel per week. On 17 July one Captain Benest announced a horse-drawn bus service; but this did not start until the following October, and then lasted only a short time, due to lack of support. In November the control of petrol supplies for civilian use was handed back to the States; stocks lasted until the following March, after which the fuel had to be imported, with the allowance being about 15,500 gallons per month. This continued until November 1944, when the civilian stock dried up, after which it was supplied 'on loan' by the Occupying Authority, for essential purposes only, until Liberation Day. 499 gallons were used in the last week of the Occupation; the Germans still had 55,000 gallons at that point, which were handed over to the States. During these last months the Germans demanded detailed accounts of the use of cars and motor cycles, and 'taxi J 9999 is to be used as an auxiliary ambulance only'; doctors were only to use their cars to visit bedridden patients. A number of buses on the road had been converted to producer gas from charcoal, and the Germans had taken control of charcoal stocks on 16 June 1942.

On 24 June 1941 the rule of the road was altered to 'keep to the right.' This does not seem to have caused much of a problem – it would not be very likely to do so, with such restricted traffic – but it did mean that bus passengers had to alight in the middle of the road.

In 1942 the Occupying Authority issued an order with regard to tyres; people who owned tyres were to inform the States Department of Transport and Communication. Serviceable and non-serviceable tyres were to be stored separately. Dr. Mortimer Evans appears to have had some problem, for the Department was informed on 6 June that he had two new tyres and two worn; he explained that the new ones had been purchased before the Occupation. At any rate, four old ones were taken away and put into store. There were, of course, severe problems in Britain at the same time over rubber products, after the Japanese invasion in the Far East.

One M. Grignand, of Caen, acted for the States over the purchase of tyres. In November 1943 he was considered to be negligent in his duty, and his employment was cancelled. At this range of time one finds oneself wondering if M. Grignand was in fact doing his bit for the Allied cause, unappreciated by the local authorities.

It was reported on 21 July 1942 that a Court Martial had

The Occupation Years

recently to pass prison sentences in several cases for careless driving of motor vehicles, and it was pointed out that, even if no accident took place, 'Immoderate speedy driving, especially in villages, will be punished.'

A letter from the German Commandant of 31 July 1941 stated that there were about thirty derelict cars at the Airport, and they were to be taken to the collection centre. It seems likely that they had been left there, and others at the harbour, by people who had left the Island hurriedly just before the German landing.

There was an order in January 1941 about lights on vehicles; headlamps were to be masked, and other lights dimmed, so as to be visible only at one hundred feet.

Macready wrote to the Department of Transport and Communications, complaining about the worn-out state of public service vehicles; repairs such as rebores could not be carried out as there were no spares. Pistons and rings were unobtainable: and while this, of course, applied to public transport traffic, it may be assumed the same applied to such cars as there were in circulation. The Germans approved of his request for a hundred lorries and ten buses for the Department.

In April 1942 the Commandant required details of all vehicles:-

1. Licensed cars.
2. Civil reserve.
3. Other serviceable cars.
4. Unserviceable cars.

He required the name of the owner, the make and horsepower of each vehicle; and its condition.

In 1943 there was an urgent appeal by the Attorney-General against an instruction to withdraw his licence from a Mr. Benest, this appeal being on the grounds of ill health. The Department's Inspector had received a visit from 'A prominent official who could not be named' saying that Mr. Benest's and Major Le Masurier's cars were unneccessary.

In November 1943 there was a complaint over the lack of bicycle lamps, and a request was made for more to be available.

In June 1944, ten motor cycles were to be requisitioned.

The Germans introduced the yellow lines which are still used at road junctions and to indicate parking restrictions. The rule at road junctions was absolute – Stop. In Guernsey apparently one was allowed to proceed at up to about 4 mph, which would allow a driver to see what might be coming. There is a story that the rule was relaxed in Jersey when the wife of a States VIP did not stop absolutely, but this may be apocryphal.

MOTOR TRAFFIC

1. Drivers of vehicles (Cars, Lorries, Motor Cycles) are notified that all Driving Permits will become invalid at midnight on September 10th. Applications for renewal should therefore be sent to the Petrol Office without delay. A new Driving Permit, after the application has been approved, will be issued only against surrender of the old one.

2. Civilian vehicles may only be used in the general public interest. Journeys which are not of absolutely vital necessity are forbidden. Vital necessity will be determined on the basis of communal interest and not on that of the interests of any single person.

3. The Island Government will control the vehicles issued with permits by means of inspection, without warning, by the Civil Police Force. Owners of cars who act in contravention of this order, especially those who misuse their Permits for private purposes (joy-riding) will be liable to a withdrawal of their Driving Permits.

4. It is strictly forbidden to dismantle cars not licensed, or to render them unfit for use by other means. Contraventions will be severely punished by the German Military Authorities.

(Signed)
J. MESSERVY NORMAN,
President of the Department of Transport and Communications.

Department of Transport and Communications

MOTOR TRAFFIC OFFICE

ON MONDAY, September 9th, 1940, in order to conserve petrol, a restricted bus service will come into operation.

The travelling public are earnestly requested to make their shopping excursions during the early part of the week and so ease the congestion on Saturdays.

When last buses have their complement, short distance and excess passengers cannot be guaranteed travel.

J. MESSERVY NORMAN,
President.
P. T. A. MACREADY,
Inspector.
Department of Transport and Communications.

9 September 1940.

Above and on following pages: notices published and documents issued during the Occupation years, 1940-45.

ORDER

concerning the circulation of civil Motor Vehicles (Motor Cars, Motor Cycles and other Motor Vehicles) dated August 15th, 1940, made on behalf of the Commander-in-Chief of the German Army, by the Chief of the Military Administration in France.

In virtue of the plenary powers conferred upon me by the Führer and Supreme Chief of the German Army, I make the following Order:

§1.

The circulation of civil motor vehicles shall not be allowed except for public utility transport, that is to say, for urgent transport necessary for essential purposes.

§2.

Civil motor vehicles shall not circulate unless the owners of those vehicles have obtained a special permit from the States Department of Transport and Communications, subject to the approval of the Field Commandant. The permit shall only be granted if the circulation is of public utility (see §1).

The permit is at all times liable to be cancelled; it must be withdrawn at the request of the Field Commandant.

§3.

The following shall be exempt from the provisions of §2:—

(a) Tractors used exclusively for agricultural purposes.
(b) Motor vehicles used by returning refugees, until their arrival at their homes.

§4.

Drivers of motor vehicles shall be bound to carry on them a certificate from the States Department of Transport and Communications relating to the permit, and they must present this certificate on demand to the competent authorities. A certificate from the States Department of Transport and Communications relating to the permit must be fixed on the motor vehicles—except motor cycles—on a clearly visible part of the inside of the windscreen. The owner as well as the driver of the vehicle shall be responsible for seeing that this is done.

§5.

Any alteration to motor vehicles, even to those not licensed under §2, which would nullify or diminish their utility, shall be forbidden.

§6.

The regulation relating to the admission of motor vehicles to public circulation remains in force.

§7.

Any person contravening the provisions of this Order shall be liable to imprisonment and a fine or to either of these penalties. Motor vehicles which, contrary to the provisions of this Order, have been used or altered, are liable to confiscation by the competent Field Commandant.

§8.

This Order comes into force on the day of its promulgation.

NOTE: The power to grant permits and to issue certificates for the purposes of this Order has, as appears by Act of the Royal Court dated October 11th, 1940, been delegated by the Bailiff, in exercise of the powers conferred upon him by the Order of the Field Commandant dated October 3rd, 1940, to the States Department of Transport and Communications.

15 August 1940.

SUPERIOR COUNCIL

Motor Vehicles, Spare Parts and Scrap Metal (Jersey) Order, 1941.

The SUPERIOR COUNCIL, in compliance with the directions of the Field Commandant, hereby orders as follows :-

1. The Department of Transport and Communications (hereinafter referred to as "the Department) :

(a) shall take possession of all motor vehicles and of all parts of motor vehicles which have been abandoned or left derelict and which are usable as such or which, not being usable as such, are useful for other purposes, and shall cause the same to be valued by a competent valuer or competent valuers;

(b) shall offer for sale to the German Purchasing Commission all motor vehicles in good condition of which possession is so taken; and

(c) shall keep full and proper records of all material of which possession is so taken and in particular of the description, condition and valuation thereof, the place where it was found, the date on which possession was taken and the manner of disposal thereof.

2. This Order shall come into force forthwith and may be cited as the Motor Vehicles, Spare Parts and Scrap Metal (Jersey) Order, 194

Approved.

SCHUMACHER,
     Colonel.

A. M. COUTANCHE.
     Bailiff.

This 14th day of May, 1941.

Above: 14 May 1941.
Opposite: 14 October 1941.
Page 68: 4 March 1942.
Page 69: 21 May 1942.

ORDER
relating to used tyres

1.) Every person having at Jersey in his actual possession or personal custody any tyre or tyres shall, within ten days of the date of this Order, declare in writing to the Department of Transport and Communications (hereinafter referred to as "the Department") the number of such tyres and the place or places where they are to be found.

2.) The Department shall take into custody all tyres to which this Order applies and shall store separately those tyres which are serviceable and those which are unserviceable.

3.) Receipts shall be given by the Department for all tyres taken into custody in pursuance of this Order and in such receipts there shall be stated—

  (*a*) the description, size and make of the serviceable tyres ; and

  (*b*) the weight of the unserviceable tyres.

4.) The Department shall keep full and proper records of all tyres taken into custody in pursuance of this Order, and, in particular, of the description, size and make of the serviceable tyres, of the weight of the unserviceable tyres, and for the names of the owners thereof.

5.) Subject to the provisions of this Order, the taking into custody of tyres in pursuance of this Order shall not in any way affect any right or interest in respect thereof which may be vested in any person.

6.) In this Order "tyre" means any used rubber cover or tube constructed for use as a tyre or part of a tyre of a motor vehicle or a bicycle, but excludes any cover or tube fitted on any wheel or spare wheel or a motor vehicle or a bicycle other than a motor vehicle or a bicycle which is totally unrepairable or which is unrepairable at the present time.

7.) Any person contravening the provisions of Article 1 of this Order shall be liable to imprisonment or a fine.

St. Helier, 14.10.1941.

The Field Commandant,

KNACKFUSS,
Commander.

Field Command 515
Az.02-19   TRANSLATION   4th March 1942   W 31/4/20

The Bailiff of Jersey.
                Traffic Regulations in Jersey.
               Ref. Conversation with Jurat Norman.

1. Traffic accidents have increased of late. The reason for this is that the speed of vehicles is too great in the built-up areas and especial in St. Helier.
     The measures given below are, therefore, to be introduced. In the first instance, however, the police must be made aware of the necessity for exercising supervision with regard to the strict execution of the Orders and for the prosecution of Offences.

II. Arranging "Stop" Streets:-
     I request that by 20th March 1942, you will arrange for "Stop" streets, i.e. paint a line on the roadway and place the international "Stop" sign in a suitable position at the following points. Wooden boards may be used for this purpose:-

1. Where St. Marks Road enters St. Saviour's Road.
2.   "   Stopford Road   "   "   "
3.   "   Tunnel Street   "   "   "
4.   "   Simon Place   "   "   "
5.   "   Green Street   "   Colomberie.
6.   "   Francis Street   "   "
7.   "   Conway   "   "   The Esplanade.
8.   ".   Roussel   "   Rouge Bouillon
9.   "   Great Union Road "   "   "
10.

III. Reduction of the speed limit in St. Helier to 27 km. (15 miles).
     Within the limits of St. Helier a speed limit not exceeding 27 km. (15 miles per hour) is hereby ordered. I request that you will give suitable public notice of this after having had signs with the German and English text "Hoechstgeschwindigkeit in der Innenstadt St. Helier 27 km. (15 miles Meilen)" "Speed limit in the Town of St. Helier 27 km. (1 miles per hour) placed at the following points:-

1. Sign on the Esplanade at the junction of Kensington Place in the direction of the centre of the town on the right hand side.

2. Sign in New Street at the corner of King Street.

. Sign in Bath Street at the corner of La Motte Street.

4. Sign in Val Plaisant, corner of Rouge Bouillon.

5. Sign in Midvale Road, corner of Rouge Bouillon.

6. Sign in Rouge Bouillon, corner of Undercliff Road.

7. Sign in Parade Place, corner of Kensington Place.

1V. Finally, I request that you will have "No Parking" boards placed in the street in front of the Victor Hugo Hotel, each approximately 30 meters from the entrance and also at the entrance and exit to the square, i.e. a total of 4 boards.

                                        For the Field Commandant,
                                            Dr. Casper, O.K.V.R.

Verordnung	Order of the 21st May, 1942
zur Durchfuehrung der Verordnung zur Regelung des Strassenverkehrs im besetzten Gebiet Frankreichs (StVO) vom 13. Maerz 1941 (VOBIF S.202). vom 21. Mai 1942.	for execution of the Order of March 13th, 1941, regarding Road Traffic in the occupied territory of France (StVO) (VOBIF page 202).
Auf Grund der mir vom Fuehrer und Obersten Befehlshaber der Wehrmacht erteilten Ermaechtigung verordne ich zur Regelung des Strassenverkehrs im besetzten Gebiet Frankreichs, folgendes:—	By virtue of the powers conferred on me by the Fuehrer and Supreme Chief of the Army and in order to regulate road traffic in the occupied territory of France, I order as follows:—
1.	1.
Amtliche Verkehrszeichen im Sinne des Par. 3 der Verordnung zur Regelung des Strassenverkehrs im besetzten Gebiet Frankreichs (StVO) vom 13. Maerz 1941 (VOBIF S.202 ff.) sind die in der Anlage aufgefuehrten Verkehrszeichen.	The road traffic signs shown in the annex shall be adopted as the official road traffic signs prescribed in Para. 3 of the Order of March 13th, 1941, regarding road traffic in the occupied territory of France (StVO) (VOBIF p. 202 and following).
2.	2.
Diese Verordnung tritt am 25. Juli 1942 in Kraft.	This Order comes into force on the 25th July, 1942.
Der Militaerbefehlshaber in Frankreich.	The Military Commander in France.

Unbeschrankter Eisenbahnübergang
Open Railway Crossing.

Verkehrsverbot für Krafträder
Closed for Motor Cycles.

Parkverbot
No Parking.

Verkehrsverbot für Fahrzeuge aller Art.
Closed to all Vehicular Traffic.

Verkehrsverbot für Kraftfahrzeuge
Closed to Motor Vehicles.

Vorgeschriebene Fahrtrichtung
Compulsory Direction of Traffic.

Verbot einer Fahrtrichtung oder Einfahrt
No Entry.

Verbot der Überschreitung bestimmter Fahrgeschwindigkeiten
Maximum Speed Limit.

Vorfahrt auf der Hauptstrasse achten!
Caution! Main Road.

Verkehrsverbot für Kraftwagen
Closed for Motor Cars.

Halteverbot
No Stopping.

Parkplatz
Parking Place.

Vorsichtszeichen
Caution Sign.

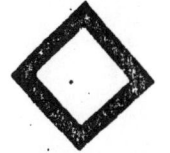

Zeichen für Hauptverkehrsstrassen
Sign for Main Thoroughfare.

DEPARTMENT OF TRANSPORT & COMMUNICATIONS.

Ref. L3/1/L.374.
EB/BLC.

TRANSPORT OFFICE.
6 BOND STREET
JERSEY, C.I.

TELEPHONE: 172 CENTRAL.
CONTROLLER: 2540 CENTRAL.

8th January 1943.

Mr. P. T. A. Macready,
Motor Traffic Office,
Library Place,
St. Helier.

Dear Sir,

    An order has been received from the Field Command, copy of which is attached, forbidding the further use of cars over 12 h.p.

    Your Car J.604 has a higher h.p. than 12., and the Department regrets it will be necessary for you to obtain something smaller.

    As soon as you have made the necessary alteration, kindly submit all particulars to this Office so that your Permit may be adjusted accordingly.

Yours faithfully,

President
Department of Transport & Communications.

8 January 1943.

The Cars Themselves

In the early days of motoring any outing was a major event. Starting the car was an exercise in itself. The petrol had to be turned on and primed, ignition timing set, and the winding handle swung – and Heaven help the man who did not hold the winder properly, for he could easily finish up with a fractured thumb or wrist if the car back-fired. The arrival of the electric self-starter revolutionised this procedure.

Maintenance was a full-time occupation – much of the work had to be done at home – but throughout the existence of the motor car this has become steadily easier. Oiling and greasing needed to be done every few hundred miles, and there was a large number of grease nipples. Techniques to ease this appeared in the 1930's: one-shot lubrication was one method, in which one central nipple distributed the lubricant to wherever it was required (when it worked properly) or 'Silentbloc' bushes, which did not need grease, but could nevertheless squeak. Today such things have virtually disappeared.

The Engine

The engine would need to be decarbonised every two or three thousand miles, and the valves reground; but this could be done at home. It would probably require reboring after about twenty thousand miles; this could not be done at home, but a garage of any size would be perfectly capable. Regrinding the crankshaft and remetalling the main bearings were other routine, if major, tasks before the war.

Engines have changed and improved considerably as the years have gone by, but retain their basic design almost without exception, which is the four-stroke function of Induction-Compression-Explosion-Exhaust. They began as single cylinder, then two cylinders, and then more and more. Four were common, but six were used in some expensive cars, which gave great increase in both power and smoothness. Eight, twelve, and even sixteen appeared on some big cars, especially in the United States, but production of the sixteen cylinders, which was on very expensive cars, did not last, while twelve and even eight cylinders became rarer; they did make for very smooth running with enormous power.

Today varying numbers of cylinders are used, from three to eight or twelve. Configurations changed from valves at the sides to valves on the top of the engine (side valves to overhead valves). The overhead valve layout was more complicated and noisier in its early days, until manufacturing techniques improved, and today practically all, if not all, internal combustion engines (in other words, the normal car's engine) have overhead valves.

Engines have become lighter through the years and this, allied to higher compression, has enabled much higher performances to be obtained from small engines. A great deal of the smoothness and quietness of the modern car is due to the silencing of the exhaust as it goes through the silencing system, and the best of engines is extremely noisy if the silencer is blown. Starting handles are no longer fitted; indeed, it would be hard to turn over a modern, high-compression engine.

Changing gear was hard work, requiring precision and double-declutching, but it was very satisfying when it went right. Devices for easing it came in the late 1920's; syncromesh appeared in 1928 from General Motors, via Vauxhall, which they had just acquired, and this obviated the need for double-declutching. The Wilson pre-selector, planetary gearbox appeared on Armstrong-Siddeley, later to be allied to a fluid flywheel by Daimler. It was totally impossible to crash this gearbox, which made a characteristic whine as it went along. The Wilson box came to be fitted on a number of makes, including Riley, MG, Talbot and a number of racing cars. Automatic gearboxes have now taken the place of all gear-changing methods apart from syncromesh.

Above: Starting handle on Rolls-Royce 20 (K Trent).
Below: Under the bonnet of a 1938 10 horse-power Talbot 10. This was a Hillman Minx side-valve engine, somewhat tuned up. (I D Wright).

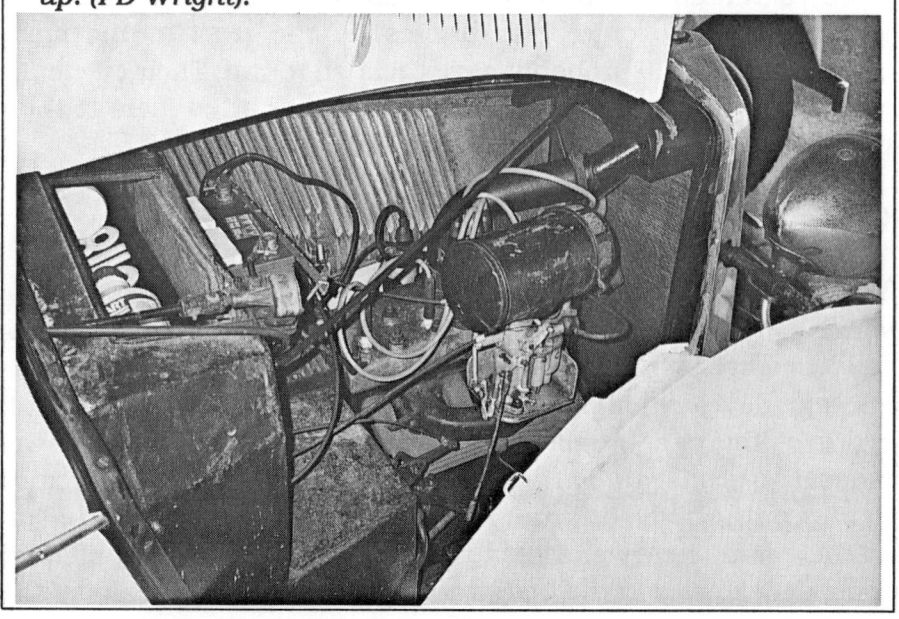

Braking

Braking improved, as it had to. The earliest brakes applied to two wheels only, and/or one on the transmission shaft, and four-wheel brakes came into general use in the 1920's. Those on early cars might be external-contracting or internal-expanding, and some American manufacturers stuck to the rather primitive former type for far too long. The brakes could be very inefficient in reverse, so a sprag would form part of the car's equipment, to be dug into the road surface on a hill to prevent the car running backwards. Early cars with four-wheel brakes carried a red triangle on the rear, to warn following traffic.

Hydraulic operation came in the 1930's, which was a dramatic improvement, but surprisingly slow to become generally adopted. This equalised braking on both sides properly; until then adjustment of the brakes had been a painstaking job. Triumph was early in this field, but Morris really was more successful. Servo-assistance featured on some cars in the early 1920's; and it was then that Rolls-Royce built under licence and improved the system fitted to Hispano-Suiza; a built-in servo assistance came with the design of two-leading-shoe brakes. Disc brakes have now become more common and effective; they are often fitted on the front wheels, with the older hub brakes on the rear; or the more expensive cars will probably have them all round. Their efficiency was demonstrated to the public when Jaguar fitted them to their cars for the Le Mans 24-hour race in 1954.

Car Bodies

There was a short-lived vogue for fabric bodies round about 1930, which were light and rattle-free, but did not last. The fabric was stretched over a padded wooden frame.

Major developments post-war have included the use of the full width of the car, by eliminating the running boards, and the monocoque construction of the body. This last has allowed greater rigidity in the body, but rust has become a more serious problem as there is no heavy chassis to provide rigidity; this had allowed some deficiencies in the bodywork. The inevitable oil leaks of the

Above: Austin 7 hood being erected in a hurry by Mrs. Pinchard. Below: Restricted rear vision in a bull-nose 1926 MG (C Forester).

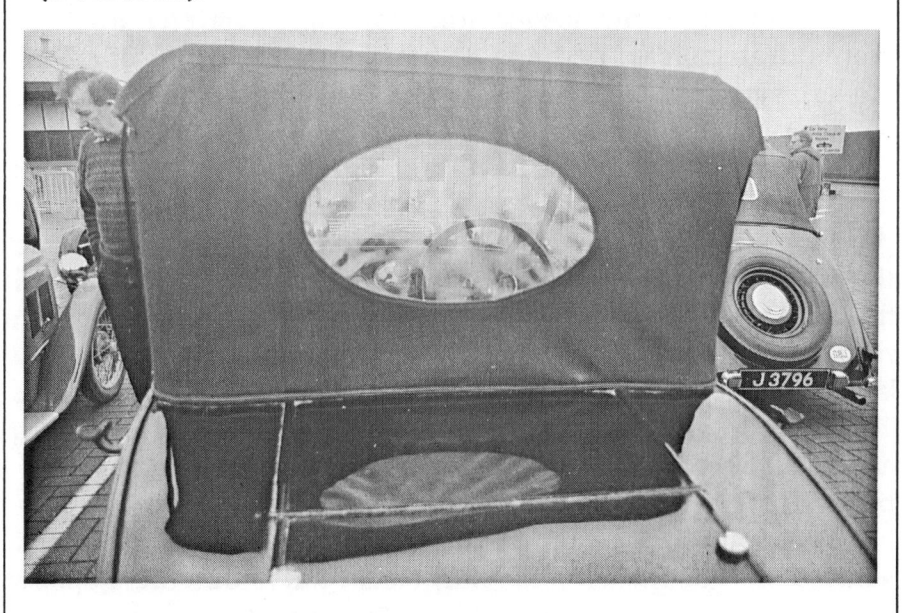

75

old days did much to protect and preserve the underside of the car; now great care is taken over rust-proofing. It is also said that the monocoque body removes all individuality from the car; but the writer remembers his Father complaining in 1937 that he could no longer recognisethe different makes of car, this *apropos* of a new Hillman Minx; and writer also remembers reading a road test report on a second-hand car which started with words to the effect that 'It is refreshing in these days, when cars are so like each other, to drive one which is different ...' This was written in 1932, in respect of a 1926 Bentley. Computers play a large part in modern car design; and if one asks two computers the same questions, one is liable to get the same answers.

The finish of the bodywork was and is important to the owner who, perhaps with his chauffeur, could be very particular about it. Paint used to be applied with great care, layer upon layer, being rubbed down between each one; finally varnish was applied; and the end result was a lovely, brilliant finish. It took ages to do this, for each coat had to dry properly before the next one could be applied, and the rubbing-down was done by hand. It would require careful maintenance, because it scratched easily, and anyway would not last indefinitely. Cellulose was a vast improvement, cutting down the time needed drastically, and giving a harder and more durable gloss, perhaps without quite the depth of colour. Modern synthetic finishes are harder and more durable, and with a deeper-still colour.

The paint, however done, is essential to protect steel coachwork, and then wax can be applied to protect the paint. It has not yet proved possible to get a surface that will repel rather than attract the dirt – that will be the day! Brightwork, brass in the early days, needed constant polishing to keep in order; nickel-plating gave a rather unsatisfactory, dull finish; and chromium plating of the brightwork transformed this aspect of bodywork maintenance. Today the brightwork may be stainless steel on more expensive cars, with a greater life expectation and no possibility of rusting or peeling off.

The most usual colour in the later pre-war days was black, which looks good when it is really clean, but shows every spot of dirt, with grey another popular finish, 'because it does not show the

Above: 4.25 litre Bentley (J Boothman).
Below: Despite the speed limit, high-performance cars like this Porsche are in demand, largely for their handling qualities.

dirt'. Strong colours, as red, green and blue, followed on. In postwar days, a great variety of colours has appeared. Newer techniques give harder and brighter surfaces. Henry Ford is reputed to have said that his customers could have any colour they liked, so long as they liked black.

Radiators and mascots

Radiators became characteristic of the various makes of car, and one could identify most of them as they came along. This has been pretty well lost since the War, though one or two manufacturers have stuck to their traditional designs, noticeably Rolls-Royce and Mercedes Benz.

Gimmicks were and are always popular. One might have had a temperature gauge on the radiator cap, or there could be a mascot, such as a bulldog, or 'Old Bill'. There were some very elegant ones, especially those made in glass by Lalique; Rolls-Royce produced their Spirit of Ecstasy to pre-empt the use of the more vulgar mascots that some people put on their cars. Some were very ugly, some were vulgar, and some were downright dangerous, and legislation now exists to prevent the use of such.

Bumpers

Bumpers were fitted to protect the fronts or backs of the cars, although some of them were flimsy enough not to give much protection, and a patent was taken out for the idea in 1905. Some owners refused to have such things, maintaining that they were only needed by bad drivers who could not judge the lengths of their cars, but they are now probably fitted by every maker. They became part of the aesthetic design, and some were held to keep the balance of the cars; they were 'harmonic stabilisers.'

Archer mascot on Pierce Arrow

Above: Boyce Motormeter (radiator thermometer) on a Bullnose MG (C Forester);
Below: Spirit of Ecstasy mascot on Rolls-Royce 20 (K Trent).

Lighting

Car lighting has improved out of all knowledge. In the early days, lights were very feeble, but were better when acetylene gas became used. There would be a container for carbide on the running board: water would have to be dripped on to the carbide to produce gas, which was then piped to the lamp; it would need to be lit by a fusee, or by a match which would blow out in any wind. Electricity must have been a godsend. Various combinations of lights were tried: side lights were placed on the front wings, on the scuttle, or inside the headlamps, which were and are usually paired.

Dazzle was controlled by different means when the lights were bright enough to demand that something be done. There was a mechanism for tilting both headlamps, by a lever operated by the driver. Next came the dip-and-switch, with a solenoid behind the nearside headlamp reflector, which tilted that reflector and extinguished the offside lamp. On some more expensive cars there could be a solenoid behind both reflectors, so that both would tilt, but leaving both headlamps alight. Various reflector materials were used, the usual one being a highly polished silvered metal, but some more expensive lamps used actual mirrors. Another system, which was favoured by Wolseley, among others, was for both headlamps to be extinguished, and pass lamps, mounted lower down on the bumper to light up. Twin filament bulbs came in the 1950's, and were fitted in both headlamps, so that both light beams dip. At the same time the design of the reflectors was more scientific, while the glasses became lensed. Between the wars, the headlamps became an important feature of the front of the car, and, in the more up-market ones, dramatically so.

Rear lights were often deplorable before the war, there frequently being only one very small light. Following uncomplimentary remarks by the Duke of Edinburgh just after the War, the rear lights have much improved, indicate the full width of the car and are backed up by red reflectors. Brake lights came in the 1930's and made a further safety feature. Lights should not only be used to see the way, but to be seen. What used to be sidelights are now just for parking and are surely not adequate on a moving car, when the driving/head-lamps need to be used.

Right: Acetylene headlamp on 1913 Buick (G Bisson); Below: Impressive Lucas headlamps and windtone horns on a 1937 Talbot BD75 belonging to the author. The passlamp has a split reflector, which had a vogue at that time.

Direction indicators

Direction indicators arrived in the 1930's. Signalling was done at first by a recognised code of hand waving; Jersey instructors often used to teach the use of a curious sign for indicating intention of stopping which could be taken to indicate 'I am going straight up in the air.' The next system used a robot arm operated manually by the driver to show his intention. Electric indicators came next; semaphore was the most usual, but the makers of Talbots, and a few others, had their own ideas, fitting arrows which lit up on the front and rear of the car to point the way. Automatic cancelling of the indicators came in the 1930's; some were on a time-switch. The present winking type came with the 1950's. Morris tried miniature traffic lights – red, amber and green – for direction indicators, but this was unsuccessful.

Windscreen wipers

Techniques for keeping the windscreen clean and clear have undergone similar improvements. At first, naturally, there were no windscreens; then, when they did arrive, the glass had to be put out of the way when it rained by opening the screen. Next the idea occurred to use a hand-operated wiper; after that, mechanical means were employed for the wiper, usually electric.

Originally there was one wiper blade, then two appeared on the more expensive cars, becoming more and more popular. At first they might require to be moved from side to side on the screen; then they hung down from the top of the screen, and later they were mounted on the scuttle. Many makers now fit wipers on the rear window. The early plate-glass windscreens were enormously heavy, becoming lighter when the screens got smaller, while the introduction of safety glass was a great saftey measure. Wiping the screen with a half-potato is a forgotten trick, which went a long way to reducing condensation and freezing on the glass.

Windscreen washers arrived mostly after the war and have now become standard equipment on cars.

Above: double windscreen wipers with built-in linkage on Lagonda (C Reynolds).
Below: Opening split windscreen and scuttle ventilators on a Bull-nose MG (C Forester).

Electric windscreen demisters were available before the War; they were rather like miniature electric fires, and must have made demands on the battery if they were left on, while not being very efficient. The other way to cope with a windscreen that misted up was to open it. Another long-forgotten dodge was that of putting rubber wedges under the trailing edge of the bonnet in heavy frost or snow, to allow hot air over the screen from the engine compartment. Post-war, keeping the windscreen glass from misting up was done by blowing warm air onto the inside, which is now standard. Demisting of the rear window is now done by heating fine wires set in the glass, and there is an increasing number of makers doing the same for the windscreen.

Heating and ventilation

In the early days of motoring the occupants were completely exposed to weather and to dust, which was considerable. Heavy clothing was the order of the day, with some sort of mask over the face and goggles. Weather protection from windscreen, hood, and then side curtains followed, and later the saloon, with side windows; these were much more comfortable.

In the early days of motoring, all cars were open, but by the 1930's the majority consisted of saloons, with the advantages of comfort. At that time they were more expensive than saloons; in 1936 an Austin 7 Opel, which was an open two-seater, cost £102.10s., while the basic Austin 7 Ruby four-seater saloon sold at £118. Sports cars were usually open, and some diehards stuck to their tourers. Today an open car is usually more expensive, whether new or old.

Heavy rugs were part of the normal equipment in the car, and foot warmers filled with hot water were sometimes found, as were footmuffs. Various methods were tried for using waste heat from the car. Attempts made to harness the heat from the exhaust pipe were not very successful. Built-in systems gradually became optional extras and are today standard fittings. Driver comfort makes for safer driving. Today's built-in heaters are much more controllable and efficient; and total air-conditioning is to be found on the more expensive cars.

The Cars Themselves

Horns

'Audible warning of approach' became desirable at an early stage. Bells and whistles were used at first, and one might have thought that the mere noise of the car itself was enough. Horns operated by squeezing rubber bulbs came into use; these might be simply utilitarian, or they could be the subject of considerable art work, and elaborate and decorative boa constrictor designs were used; these had long pipes, ending in snakes' heads, sometimes with tongues which vibrated when the horns were sounded. The next type of horn was the Klaxon, which made a vulgar noise when a button was pressed. Electric horns made life easier for the driver, and there were many of these; earlier ones made the same belching noise, but later the sounds became more refined. Peep-peep ones were found on many family cars, and 'wind-tones' were popular, usually on more up-market cars. The horns themselves might be hidden under the bonnets, but they were Heaven-sent for the accessory trade, and handsome, usually chromium-plated, ones were mounted outside. The wind-tone style lent itself to elegance, and could be fitted with trumpets of varying lengths.

A 'Letter to the Editor' on 1 March 1926 complained about noise; revellers went to two or three dances at various locales of a night, and people living near the dance halls, or garages, were 'treated to solos by the most abominable horns or hooters in the world.'

We have seen attacks by *Les Nouvelles Chroniques* on the car and driver. It resumed its assault on 18 September 1915:

> You have commented recently on the excessive speed of cars, but you should also insist that every car has an

audible warning of approach, trumpet, or horn, or anything else, to make a noise that cannot be mistaken. It is necessary, if possible, that the sounds should be uniform, and not the raucous shrieks which assail one's ears uselessly. The other day, driving my car in the country, a car passed me, like a bat out of Hell. Its horn made a noise exactly like the barking of a dog, and, hearing it, I had no idea that a car had come up behind me.

If there had been an accident, the driver would not have been held responsible. No matter how deceptive the horns might be, have not the roads been open to everyone for many years now?'

Throughout the inter-War years the motor car became more comfortable, safer, easier to handle, and better looking continuously throughout its life, and indeed this has continued since. The oft heard comment, 'They don't make them like that nowadays ...' really deserves the reply that it is probably just as well, however much one may admire or enjoy a vintage car, as does the author. The inter-war years, then, saw the car become, in today's language, user-friendly. It steadily developed into a usable article, and the 1930's, which is an era much derided by motoring historians and vintage car experts, saw it come into popular ownership. We are told that it lost come delicacy of handling with the advent of things like balloon tyres and low-geared steering, but it entered the price-range of the ordinary man (whoever he might be), and the ordinary man bought it.

The Jersey Motor Industry

An enormous industry has grown up round the car, with its manufacture, its maintenance, and, more recently, its restoration. As far as Jersey is concerned, the first of these can be dealt with briefly, since there have been no major car-building companies here. It has been seen that it was possible to build cars under licence, and it is doubtful if the number of cars so built here can ever be known. Numbers of 'specials' have been put together, particularly for competition use, but these cars were usually built from parts of existing ones. Many specials made for sand racing and other competition use come under this heading, both in the past and today. Large engines are put into small chassis, giving an enormous power-to-weight ratio. Mr. Pool was involved in producing a few cars, but it is likely that these were assembled by him from parts.

The supply of new cars however remains an important part of today's commerce. British cars were for a long time the main part of this, although French ones had a significant following; today Japanese cars have become very popular, being well-designed and well-equipped, and the makers have integrated in many cases with Western manufacturers; examples are Honda with Rover (now divorced), and Ford with Mazda. In their early days Japanese cars were lavishly equipped and comparatively cheap to buy; they probably did not have the same stamina as European-built cars, but this does not seem to be the case today.

The maintenance of cars forms a considerable proportion of commerce in the Island. A large proportion of the Jersey workforce is involved in this, and many school-leavers opt to go into the trade. Short runs, which necessarily provide most of the driving in the

Island, cause much greater wear and tear than long runs, where everything has a chance to warm up properly, and the oil to do its job. Maximum wear takes place when the car first starts up, before the oil has circulated; the engine is running on choke, which means that neat petrol is washing any oil which might be there off the cylinder walls.

Salt is disastrous to steel, and seaspray is just that to bodywork and undersides made of steel. It is always surprising to see so many cars in the layby car parks alongside Victoria Avenue in stormy weather, with sea-spray blowing over. Fortunately for cars, it is not the policy of the Jersey authorities to slosh salt onto the roads when there is any snow, although there is a certain amount of it in the grit which is laid to give a grip. Taking everything into consideration, this is perhaps the best plan, but maybe not the easiest. It is fairly uncommon for there to be heavy snowfalls in Jersey but it paralyses traffic when it does happen, and Jersey roads do seem quite unduly slippery under such conditions. The increasing use of four-wheel drive vehicles makes for greater safety and mobility in such conditions. One such occasion, among several, was on 5 January 1963, when the weather was described by the *Jersey Evening Post* as 'Arctic'; there were four centimetres of snow together with a heavy frost, the sea froze, and 'transport was almost at a standstill.'

Wear and tear, then, is on the whole greater per mile in Jersey than on the Mainland, and there is consequently a much greater proportion of newer cars here. Until recently cars were tipped into the old quarry at Mont Mado at the ends of their lives, and there must be a treasure trove, which has now been buried, if rust has left anything; this is not unlikely if oil from the sumps has been able to permeate. Nowadays they go to Bellozanne, hopefully for recycling, or for parts to be removed for re-sale and re-use.

The next section of the industry, that of restoring and preserving old cars, especially pre-war ones, is of increasing importance as interest in such cars grows. More and more of them are coming into the Island, brought by enthusiasts, and they stand out in modern traffic. It is perhaps the motoring equivalent of the antique business.

The Jersey Motor Industry

Difficult conditions outside the Union Inn, probably during the Big Freeze of 1963.

Garages

Before the 1939 War there existed numerous garages, just as there do today. Some of them came and went, some went on to become major concerns, and some were taken over or bought out by other garages. Some had agencies for manufacturers.

Until comparatively recently, repair meant just that. There was no large-scale supply of works-manufactured spare parts, or, at any rate, not as there exists today, and the local garage had to mend and make do. Reboring of cylinders and line-boring of crankshafts were within the capability of the workshop. The dreary task of remetalling main bearings was routine. Fords made a feature of their engine replacement service at remarkably low prices, even for those days before the War, and advertised it freely. The motor car has become more and more complex, and tolerance in measurements far more critical, as time has gone on.

In the early days, a repair might well be within the competence even of a blacksmith, who was indeed a highly skilled man. It could easily be that an oversize piston for one car could be found among the standard for another, and spare parts did not have to be so exact for this make of car or that only. Much of this could not be acceptable nowadays, and the use of specialist-supplied parts is essential. A lot of the work is computerised, and the system demands replacement rather that repair. Many of the electronic parts are in packages that cannot be put up locally.

Anthony's Garage in Tunnel Street was where Houillebecq's now is. It was taken over during the War by St. Helier Garages, already a large concern, which will be considered later. Work was carried out there by the staff of St. Helier Garages, and for a long time the Germans did not appreciate what was going on.

Stevenson's Garage in Gloucester Street was agent for some American cars – Chrysler, Studebaker, Chevrolet, Essex, which included Terraplane. It is suggested that Stevenson brought a fleet over, and got on with selling it. The site is now a hire car lot.

A F Gallichan, in Commercial Buildings, dealt with Morris and later Renault. It was sold to Falle's Garage when Mr. Gallichan retired, and it was then that Falle's acquired the Renault dealership.

Farnham's Garage in David Place was occupied by the Germans during the Occupation. It was later taken over by Cleveland Garages, another concern which is worth considering later.

Paragon Garage

Paragon Garage came into being early in the century, but the actual date is uncertain. It was founded by Mr. Gordon Bennett, who must have been a man of considerable drive and imagination; he was certainly eccentric. He came from a family of professinal people, but he himself refused to enter any profession. His family gave him £4,000, and told him to go away, so he came to Jersey. He and the family never met again after this, not because of any lack of desire on his part, but because of the division between trade and the professions. Paragon Garage gained agencies for Wolseley and Rover in due course, but also handled coaches, char-a-bancs, and agricultural equipment. Gordon Bennett was taken to the Petty Debts Court on 7 July 1927 by the Constable of St. Helier for the payment of £10, being the amount for which he was liable in fines, under Article 20 of the Loi sur la Voirie, for refusing to remove electric cables 'which he had erected or caused to be erected across Halkett Place and Beresford Street, and which caused obstruction to the public highway.'

Gordon Bennett drove a Model T Ford up the steps at Snow Hill, after he had modified the chassis, this in response to a challenge. At the top he received a severe reprimand from Police Sergeant Le Breton, who told him that he had broken the law (this might be questionable, as it does not seem likely that anyone would have thought to make a law banning driving up Snow Hill steps). He discussed the matter with his friends, decided that nothing had been said about driving down the steps, and promptly did just that. He died in the early 30's, but the business continued in the hands of his son, who sold out just before the War.

The family left the Island during the War, returning afterwards, when John Gordon Bennett, Bob Sangan, Earl Howe, and the JMC & LCC inaugurated the Jersey Road Race. John himself was an Old Victorian, and became a prominent racing driver, using specials, MGs, and Wolseleys, and was deeply involved with Jaguars. He

Have you seen the 2 NEW LEADERS

products of "Co-ordinated Craftsmanship"?

MECHANICAL SOUNDNESS
Overhead valve engine and 4-speed synchromesh gearbox.

COMFORT
Luxuriously roomy coachwork with anatomically correct cushions.

ACCELERATION
Overhead valves and camshaft. Lively, speedy and flexible.

SAFETY
Lockheed hydraulic braking — steady, powerful and equalised.

EASE OF CONTROL
Automatic ignition advance with supplementary hand control.

EQUIPMENT
Electric petrol gauge. Fume-extractor. 6-gallon rear petrol tank.

WOLSELEY gives *every* feature essential to complete motoring satisfaction, a new roominess and well-sprung comfort — brilliant performance — and above all an advanced technique of mechanical design that must appeal to all who value craftsmanship.

These <u>entirely new</u> conceptions of the modern car are here, in our Showrooms. Will you call and check up this "co-ordinated craftsmanship" and <u>compare values</u>.

BUY WISELY - BUY WOLSELEY
THE TRUSTWORTHY CAR

Distributed in Jersey by:

GORDON BENETT'S PARAGON GARAGES

The WASP from £165

The HORNET from £185

bought Underhill's motor engineering concern, but went to live in America in 1950.

Paragon Garage acquired a Royal Warrant when Gordon Bennett drove King George V and Queen Mary in a landaulette on a visit to the Island, at the end of which he was given a tiepin of diamonds, sapphires, and rubies. During the drive, on Grouville Hill, the Queen complained of the heat, and asked for a cushion. This was obtained from a nearby house, but later on was flung out of the car. His son drove the Prince of Wales, later King Edward VIII, on his visit to Jersey.

Varney's Garage

Varney's Garage was founded by Alfred William (Bill) Varney, who had worked for one of the Pools, in 1934, in Don Street. It became sub-agent for Austins, the main agent for the Channel Islands being in Guernsey; and it acquired the main agency for Jersey in the late 30's. During the Occupation it started doing work for the Germans, but the results of this were so unsatisfactory to them that this employment was discontinued. A number of doctors had Austins, which were kept on the road during the Occupation, providing work for the garage, which also did some for the States Essential Services. Varney himself died during the Occupation; he had a heart attack while pushing a bicycle up Mont es Croix. Incidentally, the garage repaired bicycles during the war, including making solid rubber tyres. After Mr. Varney's death, the affairs of the business passed to Mr. Wilcox, an accountant (his accountancy firm has evolved into the present-day Coopers & Lybrand). Towards the end of the Occupation, the business bought General Services Garages, which gave access to a limited liability company, and also showrooms on the Esplanade. When the lease of these showrooms ran out, premises were acquired in La Motte Street. In the early 60's, the whole concern was sold to Marshals' of Cambridge; but an absentee owner was not very satisfactory, and Cleveland Garages bought it out. This was after the fusion of Austin and Morris, with its subsequent confusion; the younger Mr Varney remembers the badge engineering which went on, and talks of cars arriving with a Morris badge on the front, and an Austin one on the rear.

The Motor Car in Jersey

Colback's Garage

Brothers James and Clifford Colback started their garage in Cannon Street in about 1930, and moved to the corner of Savile Street and Cannon Street, opening these premises on Christmas Eve 1936. It is understood that they had the agency for Swift cars; this was a make which went out of production in 1931, as a result of the great recession at the end of the 20's and the beginning of the 30's. In 1939 James Colback met Kaye Don in London, who was involved with General Motors, and, as a result, got the agency for Chevrolet cars, which were part of General Motors. He brought over a fleet of these cars, and started the Streamline Taxi Company with them; this, of course, was just before the War, and the Germans took over the fleet at the start of the Occupation. The Germans also took over the Parade Garage premises for the repair of heavy and tracked vehicles, on which they worked themselves, doing much of their welding in the street, which was closed off. They extended their working area into the neighbouring properties. Colbacks' were employed by the States on agricultural machinery, which kept them busy during the War.

Money still owed to Kaye Don for the Chevrolets was cancelled after the War. The Company still had the General Motors dealership; it acquired Wolseley, and then Opel (which was, of course, another part of General Motors) in the 1970's. It also became dealer for International Harvesters. Second-hand car dealing was a large part of the business, and a lot was done with ex-War Department vehicles, throwing away the bodies and mounting wooden truck ones: this is enough to break the heart of a motoring historian. Colt (later Mitsubishi), Audi NSU, Volvo, and SEAT became part of the empire. The company has left Savile Street for larger premised on Queen's Road, having agencies for Volvo and SEAT, but remains in the same family at present. There is a branch in Guernsey, dealing especially with the Audi agency.

La Motte Garage

La Motte Garage was founded in 1922, and acquired the Ford agency in 1928; it was just about this time that the Model T, which had been very popular, went out of production, and the Models A and B were introduced after a short delay. The business was originally owned by Bougourd Brothers of Guernsey, but later on by a Mr. Lionel Noel. It was in financial difficulty in the mid 30's, so Mr. William Sutton, who was a representative for Ford, on the agricultural side, for the West of England, Wales, Scotland, and the Channel Islands, bought it, with a colleague, to protect Ford's interest. He took delivery of several Ford V8s, which simply did not sell; so he founded Luxicabs, which took the V8s off his hands; effectively, he sold them to himself.

Cab drivers on the ranks were distinctly not happy about Luxicabs, and there were instances of sugar being put in the petrol tanks. When the Germans were requisitioning cars during the Occupation, Sutton represented the interests of the States against the requisitioning committee, whose head was in fact the Ford main agent for Germany. His job was to see that the car owners got fair value, although this was in German marks, which were redeemed after the end of the Occupation. During the War he was sent to Panhard & Levasseur, who were experts in producer gas fuel, to obtain Gasogene units for Jersey buses. After the war, he restarted Luxicabs. La Motte Garages took delivery of only fourteen new cars during the first post-war year; unlike other manufacturers, Ford regarded Jersey as part of the home market.

One remembers the vacuum-operated windscreen wipers, which went slower and slower the greater the load on the engine, especially when overtaking, the six-volt electrics, and the transverse front spring, which meant that, certainly as far as the bigger cars were concerned, they would go like bats out of Hell in a straight line, but they would not corner.

Henry Ford was a very obstinate man, and held on to some outdated ideas for a long time. Despite these vagaries, the product was a first-class car, which, like many others seems to have inspired affection not least by its faults. Fords were extremely good value for money, and the company used this fact as a basis for its advertisements in the British press, suggesting that one could have one big and one small Ford for the price of one car of other makes. This was probably true, but did depend perhaps on what the other makes might be.

It must be remembered that the commercial side was a very profitable line, with lorries, vans, and tractors.

After the War one saw the arrival of the Consul, Zephyr, Capri, and the best-selling Fiesta. Today the garage remains in the ownership of the same family. The Ford motor car has gone way up market from the old days, and today produces a wide range, the most basic being above the bottom of the market, the largest a luxury car, and the new Probe aiming at the high-performance market. La Motte Garage has recently built a new, super-complex at Sion.

St. Helier Garages

St. Helier Garages Ltd. came into being on 14 February 1920, the first board meeting being held two days earlier. A history of the business was published in 1974. There was already a company in existence, run from Bulwarks House in St. Aubin, but it is uncertain how long it had been so, and the minute books have now been lost. It 'carried on the business of a Hirer and Repairer of Motor Cars Lorries Motor Coaches Taxi Cabs etc at St. Aubins under the style of "St. Aubin's Motor Coach and Car Company."' This company was probably in financial trouble, and Mr. Frederick Anderton bought it up; the new Company had a nominal capital of £20,000. It had operated motor coaches and even motor boats, one Mr. Harold Briginshaw being one of the drivers.

The company ran several vehicles, some motor and some horse-drawn: there was a Maxwell 'touring car' which the history suggests was a form of coach, but, of course, 'touring car' was a perfectly normal description of a car of the day. There were also a Maxwell truck, a Studebaker, a Ford truck and a Ford touring car, two landaulettes (it would have been nice if they had been identified), some char-a-bancs, a motor boat, and several horse-drawn vehicles. All this looks as if the company had been very well-established.

A Mr. Nell was in the chair of the new company. A property at 37 Bath Street was bought for £3,700, of which Frederick Anderton advanced £3,000. In 1924 Harold Briginshaw was made managing director and secretary. In the same year the garage became

St. Helier Garage in Bath Street. Above picture is pre-war, when Jaguar was still S S Jaguar. Below picture is post-War, and shows General Montgomery's Humber.

The Motor Car in Jersey

agent for Clyno, which was another victim of the recession at the end of the 1920's. There was an advertisement in the *Jersey Evening Post* in 1925 'To cut a long journey short – try a Clyno; price from £175.' In 1925 a Bowser petrol pump appeared; the petrol would have had to be hand pumped. Agencies for Standard cars and Imperial motor-cycles were also acquired. In 1929, 37 Bath Street was renumbered as 87, and further agencies were added. Electricity was laid on early by the go-ahead concern, and this allowed the use of electrical equipment.

Two further branches were opened, one at First Tower in 1934, which was used for commerical and agricultural purposes, and the other at Don Road in 1932. Morgan and Singer were added to the franchises, and the first Talbot went through the Garage. Austin, Armstrong-Siddeley, S.S. (the presursor of Jaguar), Riley and Wolseley appeared on the list. Garages in those days were not confined to handling one make.

Harold Bree, the works manager, remained at that post throughout the War, and succeeded in making a profit of £30,000. Some work was carried out in what had been Farnham's Garage, out of sight of the Germans. The staff was required to sleep in St. Helier Garage just before the Liberation, in case of invasion by the British. An unpublished war-time diary has recently come to light. It tells us that St. Helier Garages had £3,000-worth of cars commandeered – 'of the 20 h.p. class' – at the start of the Occupation.

Leonard True entered the sales department in 1934, when the garage held agencies for S.S., Standard, and the Rootes Group, which had added Sunbeam and Talbot to its organisation on 1 January 1935. It did not then have the franchise for Rolls-Royce and Bentley, which came in 1956; the few Rolls-Royces in the Island at that time seem to have been brought in by their purchasers. It did have franchises for Aston Martin, Lagonda, and Frazer-Nash-BMW, which after the War became Bristol. In 1952, Mr. True made a special journey to the Rolls-Royce showrooms in Conduit Street, to acquire a car for the Duke of Leeds.

Mr. True himself had left the Island to join up in the British forces immediately the war broke out; he finished up as a POW in Burma, with dysentery, and finally returned to Jersey severely emaciated. He retired after 48 years' service to the garage, having

You must try the New

HILLMAN MINX

WONDERFUL PRICE REDUCTIONS
and another 20 New Features.
New Economy — over 40 m.p.g.
In practical tests.

SAFETY SALOON

£163

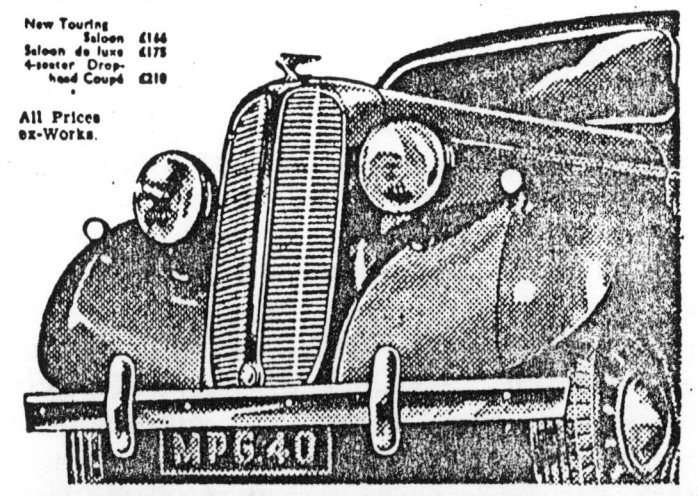

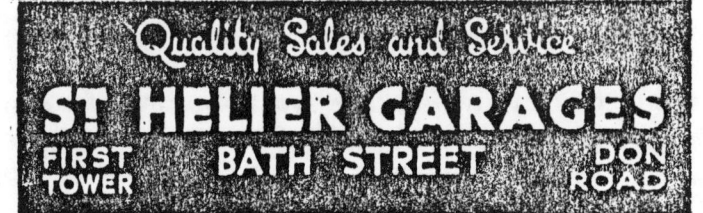

New Touring Saloon £166
Saloon de luxe £175
4-seater Drop-head Coupé £210

All Prices ex-Works.

Quality Sales and Service

ST HELIER GARAGES

FIRST TOWER — BATH STREET — DON ROAD

acquired the reputation of being able to sell ice creams to Eskimos. He became a director of the Company before he retired.

Harold Briginshaw said he would stay when the Germans arrived during the War, but in fact left. Anderton said that he would not have Briginshaw back at the end of the War, but died during the Occupation, leaving his widow in the Chair. Meanwhile, Briginshaw had made valuable contacts while he was away, so was welcomed back when the time came. Mr. Anderton's son, Brigadier W D Anderton, became chairman in 1948.

The company was sold to Mr. John Habin in 1972. St. Helier Garage and Cleveland Garage now both belong to A. de Gruchy & Co, and are being integrated. It has agencies for Rolls-Royce, Bentley, Jaguar and Daimler, Land Rover, and Lotus. All the old depots have been disposed of, and there are now showrooms in La Motte Street, and very modern workshops and showrooms in premises at Havre des Pas which had previously belonged to Cleveland Garage. It has recently been awarded a national certificate for quality service, BS5750.

Cleveland Garage

Cleveland Garage was founded by a builder, W J Ryan, who seems to have been quite an entrepreneur, at Havre-des-Pas. It had a Ford agency at first, and then Nuffield, which included Morris and its sidekicks – MG, Wolseley, Morris Commercial, and later Riley. After the war, a son, Dennis, took over a depot in David Place, and also acquired premises at Mont à l'Abbe. In October 1949 there was an outbreak of fire; this was one of a series, and evidence of arson was found, since the alarm had been raised early, with the fire quickly quenched. A Dr. Firth was called by the Defence Committee, together with two Scotland Yard detectives; and a few days later the *Evening Post*, together with some other businesses, offered a reward of £1,000 for information leading to the arrest of the arsonist.

The Nuffield agent in Guernsey was associated for some time.

It has been mentioned that Cleveland took over Varney's Garage after the amalgamation of Nuffield and Austin. This is also now part of the empire of A. de Gruchy.

Considerable reorganisation and rationalisation are under way for the group, and, if plans come to fruition, the present Cleveland showrooms in La Motte Street will become part of the St. Helier Garage complex, with its workshops; Cleveland will be entirely at the top of Queen's Road, and the present Havre-des-Pas workshops will be unconnected with motoring. This will make each concern into a much more manageable unit.

Falle's Garage

Falle's Garage was started in 1926 in Norcott Road, where Moody's upholstery business is now, and moved to Bagot Road in 1936; the founder was Jean Falle, who had previously worked in Plymouth and at Paragon Garage. It was at that time an engineering garage, which meant it had its machine shop, as did any garage of any size, and did its own reboring etc. It generated its own electricity until 1955, with a diesel engine. It acquired a Renault sub-agency, and then bought Gallichan's Garage, which gave it the main agency. It also bought a business in Guernsey, which had the Vauxhall agency in that Island; and Vauxhall offered Falle's the Jersey agency when new premises were built at Longueville. The company opened a small filling station by the Airport; business expanded as the Airport expanded, and it became a retail outlet for Ford and Citroen.

The present Mr. John Falle joined his Father in 1955, and started the hire car business with a few cars at the Bagot Road branch. The company now has about 1,500 hire cars in this Island, 400-500 in Guernsey, and about 200 in Southampton. It is another garage business which has recently opened a new super-facility, and holds several franchises, including Vauxhall, Renault, Fiat, and Ford.

Roberts' Garage

Roberts' Garage came into being in March 1955, and big Jubilee celebrations are planned for 1995. It started at Grouville, at Frank Roberts' home, doing hire and taxi work. Five years later, in 1960, a petrol station was started up in Kensington Place, providing petrol through a hole in the wall, using an old-fashioned hand-operated pump. At this time the firm ran private hire cars, including a Rolls-Royce Phantom III landaulette and Armstrong-Siddeleys, plus two hearses. However, this side of the business was not profitable, and it was given up. The garage business was extended, giving service from 07.00 hours until midnight. This garage achieved a place in the *Guinness Book of Records*, for the most petrol sold in 24 hours.

Another depot was taken over in 1978, in Springfield Road. Exhaust systems and tyres were already supplied from here, but this side of the business was further developed. A major rebuilding took place in 1994, and it is another 'state-of-the-art' depot.

Another unit was taken over in 1984 on the Inner Road, near Bel Royal, and has been developed for petrol, car-washing, and accessories. A garage at Greve d'Azette was bought in 1992, after being rented for some time, and is also a supplier especially of tyres and exhausts. The company also owns a petrol-and-accessory place at Pontac, and a small petrol depot at Gorey.

Melbourne Garage in St. John is the agent for Ferrari. It started as a small repair shop, owned by a Mr. ('Mousie') Coutanche, who built it up. It was then bought by Mr. Alex Cook, who owned Linton's garage, and was a motoring enthusiast. In 1973 it acquired agencies for Fiat, Alfa Romeo, and Lancia; Jensen and Daf were added, as were Datsun, Colt and Daihatsu.

Jackson's Garage, which used to be on the Esplanade, had a sub-agency for Austins, and then the agency for Mercedes-Benz, which it found far more interesting; it gave up the Austin franchise, but acquired BMW. It is now situated on the Rue de Pres Trading Estate.

The Jones family was involved in the business for many years. Grandfather began at Thompson's Garage in Bath Street, and then started up for himself in St. Mark's Lane, in part of a stables premises; later he transferred to Phillips Street. The garage moved to Five Oaks in 1937, with a nine-year lease; this length of lease could be arranged with a minimum of bother, but a longer one had to go through the Royal Court. It did not have any agencies, concerning itself with dealing and repairs. The Five Oaks Garage would handle any make of car, and St. Saviour's Hill was used as a test hill; 'No, I don't believe you could have come up in top gear.

The family left the Island during the war, and worked on aircraft engineering, while the premises were used by the Germans. The Jones family returned after the War, but is now out of the business, and the Five Oaks Garage has the agency for Porsche, which it had in the Jones' time, Audi, and also Volkswagen, which is associated with Porsche.'

There was a number of other garages in the country, and today many still exist, which give immensely valuable local service. Some have remained in the same family ownership for very many years, and give a very personal service. Mr. Syvret, who had a business at La Moye which he ran in a highly individual manner, has recently died. Some of these country garage businesses are not all that small, such as perhaps Augres Garage, which handles Toyotas, or Bel Royal Garage, that has the Mazda agency.

There were two Pools who gave their names to businesses; G H, on the corner of Don Street, was agent for Essex and its subsidiary Terraplane, while J.B. had no agency.

Richmond's Garage, next to West's Cinema, now West's Centre in Bath Street, was commercially orientated, handling International lorries and tractors.

Frank le Sueur's Garage, which dealt with Renaults, had its site taken over by C.I. Auto Spares.

Bougourd's Garage in La Motte Street, is now a show-room for St. Helier Garages.

Barnes' Garage was founded in 1912 by Mr. Bert Barnes, who had learned his trade in America, and the business still remains in the same family, functioning in Devonshire Place. When Bert Barnes came back to the Island from America there were said to be six cars in the Island. The concern handled at one time Vauxhall, Bedford, and Citroen, but will, of course, deal with any make.

Another one which came and went was New Street Motors, opposite Vauxhall.

Primrose Garage, on the Esplanade, dealt only with coaches and char-a-bancs.

Goldsmith's Garage, on Victoria Avenue, did a roaring trade in petrol up to the time that Victoria Avenue became twin track, when, following an argument with Island Development Committee, the proprietor complained of loss of business, and left the Island for Australia, apparently in some dudgeon. The premises were left to rot.

The Dunlop Tyre Company had a depot in Oxford Road.

Linton's Garage on Victoria Avenue occupied a prime site, which is now occupied by la Motte Garage.

There was a couple of scrap merchants for cars; Getin had one in Ingouville Place, and Picot had the other in Providence Street.

A reference has been made of the growth of the hire car business, which increased enormously in the 80's. It was nothing new, except in its volume. It was considered desirable to be able to recognise traffic which might well not be very sure of its whereabouts, so it became mandatory for hire cars to carry red H plates. In theory, this should be a good thing, so that one can make allowance for visitors' uncertainty; but drivers of hire cars frequently complain bitterly that local motorists pressurise them unmercifully; resident drivers notice this particularly when they have occasion to drive H cars. It would be well to remember one's own problems in picking the correct lane in strange cities, and give consideration to strangers' similar difficulties in Jersey, particularly with the new complex round the Esplanade and Harbour area, and at the eastern end of the Tunnel.

The Jersey Motor Industry

Advertisements

Advertising in the local press does not appear to have hit the high spots of national advertising, but the object has been the same. There was a Guernseyman who placed these lines in the Guernsey Press: 'For sale a second-hand car. Would grace any nobleman's garage. Complete with spare wheel and tyre to fit'. Cars with which he dealt were likely to have been 'bangers'.

On January 1 1935 the following advertisement appeared in the *Jersey Evening Post*:

> 15.9 Austin 1935 model for sale.
> Has only done 200 miles.
> Owner Driver.
> First offer of £180 secures.

The advertiser had an address in Town, and one may wonder what lay behind the sale by a private individual of such a car. Someone else advertised in the same issue for a Morris car or van, which 'has to be cheap'. Other firms inserted under the small advertisements motoring accessories, such as:

> Car starter batteries 19s.6d.,
> Welsh cord tyres from 18s.6d.

and so on. (Another advertisement in the same issue was inserted by the pharmacist de Faye, for his ginger wine, 'New price 1/6 per 1 pint bottle)

The main advertisements in the local press were and are those of the large garage concerns, and St. Helier Garages appear to have been the biggest advertiser in pre-war days. In retrospect some ethics were observed, which does not seem to happen today. It was fair to say how much better one's own wares were than the others, but one did not actually name the other, lesser, makes to their detriment, as now happens. Locally advertisers did not use pictorial blocks until about the mid-20's, when illustrations of cars began to be used.

Some advertisements are appended. It would not be quite true to say that they were taken completely at random, as we have seen that St. Helier Garages were much the most frequent advertisers.

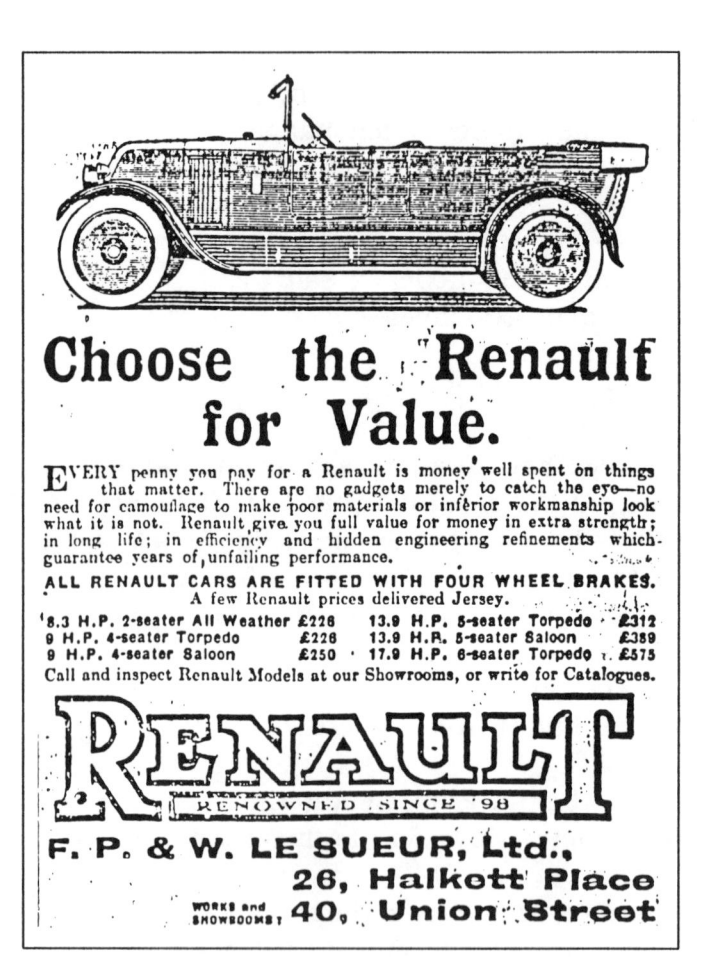

Choose the Renault for Value.

EVERY penny you pay for a Renault is money well spent on things that matter. There are no gadgets merely to catch the eye—no need for camouflage to make poor materials or inferior workmanship look what it is not. Renault give you full value for money in extra strength; in long life; in efficiency and hidden engineering refinements which guarantee years of unfailing performance.

ALL RENAULT CARS ARE FITTED WITH FOUR WHEEL BRAKES.

A few Renault prices delivered Jersey.

8.3 H.P. 2-seater All Weather	£226	13.9 H.P. 5-seater Torpedo	£312
9 H.P. 4-seater Torpedo	£226	13.9 H.R. 5-seater Saloon	£389
9 H.P. 4-seater Saloon	£250	17.9 H.P. 6-seater Torpedo	£575

Call and inspect Renault Models at our Showrooms, or write for Catalogues.

RENAULT — RENOWNED SINCE '98

F. P. & W. LE SUEUR, Ltd.,
26, Halkett Place
WORKS and SHOWROOMS, 40, Union Street

Roads and Fuel

The Highways

At the start of the nineteenth century roads did not exist in Jersey. In November 1788 one Richard Monck ran a bus service between St. Helier and St. Aubin, using the beaches, 'tide permitting.' The bus was, of course, horse-drawn. In 1866 the buses between Town and St. Aubin ran every thirty minutes, and the fares were 3 pence and 4 pence. There were twelve cab stands; the fares were one shilling for the first mile, and sixpence for every fraction of a mile thereafter; this seems very expensive in terms of the contemporary money value. In the early 1800s the Lieutenant-Governor, General Don, constructed roads, radiating from St. Helier, for military purposes; the Island was at that time of strategic importance.

Bonsor has written about the formation of the Jersey railway system, and the many problems and hiccoughs associated with it; in 1872 there were horse-drawn buses running in connection with it. In 1910 a second-hand Straker-Squire omnibus came on the scene, running between St.Helier and St. Aubin. Horse buses were still present in numbers; there was a yellow one, known as the Orange Box, and another called Hallelujah, which was owned by a member of the Salvation Army. An English company, the Devon Motor Transport Company, brought over a fleet of buses, calling itself the Jersey Motor Transport Company, and this was the beginning of the end for the trains. The first JMT motor bus arrived 2 April 1923, and was registered J 958; it was said to be capable of 10 mph, and to have the comfort of a car. The Eastern Railway gave up without a struggle, but the Western Railway kept going, even running its own buses; it then bought the JMT in 1928.

Winter train services ceased in 1932, and there were road services only by 1935. The promenade along the sea edge from St. Helier to St. Aubin and the Railway Walk, together with the remnants of stations, remain from the Jersey Western Railway, and the Parish Hall at St. Aubin used to be an important station, which was destroyed by fire, together with a lot of the rolling stock, in 1936. A few remnants of the Eastern Railway can also be seen, as the old station at Pontac, and some of the cutting at Gorey.

By the end of 1923 the JMT had a fleet of five solid-tyred buses; pneumatic tyres were fitted in 1925, and this must have made a dramatic difference in passenger comfort. There had been difficulty in keeping the solid tyres on the wheels. The minimum fare was 2d. (about one penny).

Roads themselves were surfaced with cracked stones and gravel, levelled by steam rollers, and repaired with the same material up to the mid-1920's; rate-payers in country parishes were required to provide the labour. Wood paving did appear about 1910, and concrete and tarmacadam about 1930; otherwise the surfaces were mud in wet weather; this is remembered in the street name of Rouge Bouillon. The concrete was prepared from ashes from the St. Helier destructor. In all, Jersey is estimated to have about six hundred miles of road.

Les Nouvelles Chroniques de Jersey did not like the motor car. It published a broadside on 3 June 1903:

> It is time that legislation took particular notice of motor cars and bicycles. These machines become absolute demons on the main roads. One cannot cross the street without running the risk of being knocked over by this new means of travel, which is increasing year by year. The new invention is an outrage. Petrol-bicycles are even more dangerous than the cars themselves, or pedal-powered bicycles ... People who use these machines give warning of their approach by touching a little instrument attached to the machine which emits a horrible sound, like a siren, which, instead of lessening, increases the danger to pedestrians ... We say that cars and motor cycles should be forbidden in Town. We

have not got big roads, like London and Paris....Nursemaids with prams are in danger ... We recently saw a car go down Burrard Street – a narrow street, which is difficult enough for pedestrians on Saturdays – making a frightful noise, which scared coach-horses; and, on going into Halkett Place, went at a speed which gave rise to comment ... Petrol-driven bicycles are a greater menace than Football ... We demand protection for the public which it does not have at present ... No amusement should threaten public safety ... We no longer see why motorists should be exempt from taxation. Dog owners pay taxes, as do those who hire out horses, and a tax on motorists would have two good results; it would add to revenues, and it would probably prevent the too-rapid increase in the number of machines. Here is our idea: we put a tax of five pounds sterling on every car. Every car should carry a number and every driver should have a licence ... Up to now, thanks be to God, no accident has so far happened to cause loss of life ...

This provoked a reply from 'Riviere':

Monsieur; permettez-moi de vous dire que votre article de fond de 3 Juin ne rencontre pas mon approbation.

He goes on:

To say that cars and bicycles become absolute demons on the roads is an assertion ridiculous in the highest degree ... A fair tax would be very difficult ... The motor car is the means of locomotion of the future ...
    Agreez, Monsieur, mes salutations empressees.

Strong words! The *Nouvelles Chroniques* renewed its attack on 6 May 1905:

The danger to the public of Jersey from automobiles increases all the time. In England accidents caused by these cars happen daily ... statistics ... not less than a thousand, some causing death ... Various reasons; the temptation to drive at too high a speed, or the driver or chauffeur does not know his job ... or some fault in the construction of the car. Lastly, the noise made by the hooter which sometimes looks like a serpent ... which frightens horses or those who cannot hear. The foghorn on the Casquets does not give greater shock to the ears in a more maddening manner than the horns of cars. Worse still, when the car is stationary in the road the noise does not cease ... They are dangerous to the public safety, either in St. Helier or in the country ... We have just seen an example in St. Peter, where a collision between a car and a carriage has killed a valuable horse and seriously injured the occupant of the carriage ... We know that this a a new fashion ... We do not understand why bicycles should be exempt from taxation ... We write in the common interest; no amusement should put the public in peril.

On 29 January 1912 the Viscount, R R Lempriere, Seigneur of Rozel, was fined fifteen shillings for leaving his car unattended for seven hours in the Royal Court Road. He refused to pay this, maintaining that the road was a private one, and the road authority had no jurisdiction. The Constable of St. Helier, J E Pinel, agreed that he was in error, and amended the fine to five shillings, under the law Encombrement des Routes; he insisted that the road was the property of the States, and therefore not private, and 'any person is forbidden to allow a charette which he drives to stand in the streets of St. Helier.'

The Viscount did not take this lying down, and claimed that his car was not a charette, since that was a two-wheeled vehicle with shafts. The Constable argued that the term 'charette' covered all vehicles, and the Viscount finally paid the five shillings. It was reported on 29 January 1947 that there had been a severe frost, and Mr. E Queripel had had a skid on his motor cycle, which finished up on top of him and his pillion passenger; however, both were uninjured. There was a 'few minor car accidents.'

Roads and Fuel

2.6 litre Lagonda outside Samarés Manor, about 1951.

Petrol

Mr. Peter Falla of St. John's had to have his petrol brought in on the ketch *Mizpah*, and that St. Helier Garage had a Bowser pump in 1925. Mr. Carre at St. Ouen's Garage had a pump by 1931, and we are told that Mr. Dolbel had the first one at La Moye. These would have been hand-operated pumps, in which the liquid was pumped into a sight glass or a glass container, and it ran from there into the car, this at the rate of one gallon at a time. A pump of this sort can be seen in the Jersey Motor Museum. Before the advent of the pump, petrol would have been supplied in some sort of can; one distributor, for instance, would get his stock of Pratts' Petrol from a store in St. Helier, in two-gallon cans, and then deliver it to his customers. Mr. Goldsmith got his from Russia in forty-gallon drums. Commercial organisations had to store petrol in officially-approved stores, because of fire risk.

In 1930 Shell petrol cost 8d. per gallon (old money, about 3p. today). Just before the War a gallon would have cost about 9.5d (about 4p), and the price went steadily up after the War to about 1/6d (7.5p) in the early 50's. We have recently learnt that the cost of the actual petrol is much higher in Jersey than in the UK, but the tax is a good deal lower, so that the net result is lower. On the mainland, successive Chancellors of the Exchequer have used increases of petrol and car taxation as a means of raising more revenue. This is supposed to combat inflation by putting up the cost of transport, which is a fundamental part of our economy, but the logic is difficult to understand to a simple mind. The 1994 Jersey Budget introduced a duty on petrol of 10.26p a litre for leaded and 7.21p for unleaded fuel, which compare to £36.14 and £31.32 in the UK, and 8p and 6.1p in Guernsey for the same, but has to provide revenue that previously came from the annual road tax as well as that which always came from petrol tax.

In the early 30's lead was added to petrol to cut down pinking, which is premature ignition in the cylinders. This was successful. At the same time the octane rating of the fuel was steadily rising, or, in other words, the petrol was getting 'hotter.' This allowed increase in the compression ratio of the engines, which gave improved performance. In the last few years, it has become apparent that the level of lead in the atmosphere has become excessive, which is thought to cause mental problems such as lowered intellect, and that this excess is due to the steadily increasing amount of motor traffic putting out lead in the exhaust fumes. Engines are now made so that they will function satisfactorily without lead in the petrol; some older engines may have their ignition retarded so that they can do without it, although this may affect the performance. Valves and valve seats suffer from unleaded fuels if they do not have the benefit of modern metallurgical advances.

Techniques for delivering petrol to the engine are in the process of change. Traditionally, the carburettor was the means; in the very early days, it gave a constant supply, and the speed had to be adjusted by the gears, but very soon the carburettor was able to vary the amount of petrol going into the cylinders. Supercharging had a vogue, especially for very high-performance and racing cars, but it was very extravagant and expensive, so was not for the ordinary motorist: it involved forcing the petrol and air mixture into the cylinders. It is however beginning to make a reappearance. Carburettors improved, and in the last few years have been superseded in the more expensive cars by fuel injection, giving more accurate delivery of petrol to the engine, with improvement in both performance and economy. Turbo-charging is another recent innovation, using the pressure of the exhaust gases to drive the blower to give a dramatic up-rating in performance. Turbo-charging is particularly useful for a diesel engine.

Before the War a garage forecourt would have petrol pumps for many of the petroleum companies, but since then the tendency has been for one-franchise-only representation, apart from very large depots, such as those on the motorways in Britain. Diesel fuel is today becoming more in demand. If the engine is properly adjusted, it burns cleanly, but gives an inferior and noisier performance. With help, however, as from a turbocharger, the performance returns; but extra noise still remains, although this is improving with newer engines. The fuel is cheaper, largely owing to lower taxation, and the engine using it has a much longer life (Jersey tax 7.32p per litre). Initial cost of a Diesel-engined car is higher, but the net result is a considerable saving for the high-mileage user.

Other means of providing power are being worked on, although not so much is heard now as there was a few years ago, when the Arab oil-producers first discovered the value of their oil, and put up the cost to what seemed a sky-high level. Hydrogen is one alternative; electricity is another, and some mention of it will be made later. Renault is at present talking of liquefied petroleum gas; this couples economy with clean burning. Gas from sewage is another subject for investigation. Alcohol made from sugar beet was tried once upon a time in France; it might be expected that cars should run sweetly on it.

Queen Street, February 1936; G L Benest's Estate Agents, Valuers and Auctioneers. The American car parked outside has a Birmingham Registration.

The Motor Car in Jersey

We have seen that by 1915 there were only 500 cars, and this had increased to 11,000 just before the start of the 1939 War. This may sound a lot, but they were not all out at the same time. The real explosion in numbers came after the Occupation.

In Jersey in the 20's and 30's, as on the Mainland, the small family car was popular. Cars were taxed on their horse-power, which discouraged big engines, and also led to long-stroke, comparatively inefficient ones. People just did not like paying annual car taxes any higher than they could help, but, despite that, American cars were astonishingly popular; as they were big and glamorous. They sold well. The British car was built for the British road conditions, and Jersey was very similar. The same cars were common, with abundant Morrises, Austins, Hillmans and Fords. Continental makes were less common, with Renault probably the most usual. Model T Fords had been well-liked, but, as has been mentioned, the Ford V8 did not sell well.

It is interesting to look through the registers of cars from the inter-war years in the old Motor Tax Department, and to see the spectrum of makes. Many of them have now disappeared, although a number was still there in the early post-war era. One may regret the passing of many famous names, since there was considerable marque loyalty; but sentiment is not enough for big business. Many of those names remain in the ownership of the major manufacturers, and may appear as variants of standard offerings, like Daimler; MG and Bentley are names which are reappearing in their own rights.

Official Cars

There appear to be no records of the cars that were run by Government House for official use before the War; but a Daimler is remembered, 'of the Queen Mary type'. This could make it a Hooper-bodied car with a very high roof-line, and it might have been a double-six or a twenty horse-power one. A report of a Daimler 36 horse-power being shipped out of the Island in 1959, might have been the same one; and there was certainly a royal blue Humber Snipe. During the Occupation Government House was served by one or more of the Wolseleys brought in by Gordon Bennett, and also a red Mercedes-Benz 190, with the registration J1000. This car was around for some years after the War, and was followed by an Armstrong-Siddeley Sapphire limousine, and then by two successive Daimler type DS 420 limousines.

It is obviously important that the official car should be a prestige model, and one should be able to enter in dignity without removing one's top hat. The Government House limousine did not and does not carry a number plate, but wears an illuminated Crown when on official duty: the numbers J2 and J4 are allocated to Government House, for the personal cars of the Lieutenant-Governor. J 4 did not pay road tax when it applied, but it seems that J 2 did. Just before the War, Government House had J 14 and J 28 on a Wolseley 14 and Hillman Minx respectively.

Curwood's

The Curwood firm was founded in 1892 by the present Mr. Curwood's grandfather, as a Carriagemaster business, providing horse-drawn vehicles to undertakers for funerals, until 1943. The horses finally went then as it had become impossible to feed them. Motor cars were introduced just after the First World War, the contemporary Mr. Curwood having been wounded in both arms, and being unable to handle his horses. The first motor hearse in the Island was a Daimler, with two-wheel brakes, and a handbrake on the carden shaft (the propeller shaft). Six Wolseley landaulettes were brought over for the Prince of Wales' visit in 1936 by Paragon Garage, and Curwood's bought three of them afterwards. They were requisitioned by the Germans at the start of the Occupation, but other cars were hidden round the stables, which were in Palmyra Road. There were two Daimler hearses and three Humbers, and these were brought back into use after the War, having been reassembled after their wartime dismantling.

Above: Curwood's Austin Princess outside St. Brelade's Church. Opposite: Curwood's Daimler; photograph taken for submission to Buckingham Palace prior to Royal visit to Jersey when this car was used.

The Motor Car in Jersey

Since the end of the War, the firm has gained momentum, and at the present time has six Daimlers, five of them being limousines and one a hearse, two Humber Snipes, four Van Den Plas Princess limousines and a hearse, and a Daimler 104 Majestic Major. These cars are on stand-by for Government House and all sorts of ceremonial work for the States, as well as private hire work of any sort.

If one had a similar car to any of those used by or for Government House, one stood a fair chance of being saluted by the Police as one drove up King and Queen Streets. Something like this certainly happened in the days when Government House had its Armstrong Siddeley Sapphire. The Lieutenant-Governor was expected at St. Ouen, and someone was put to watch out for his car, when Mr. J J Le Marquand came along in his own Sapphire saloon. What followed was pretty well inevitable; after all, the Armstrong Siddeley Sapphire was not a car seen very often.

This puts the author in mind of a time in Italy, driving a Rolls-Royce Silver Cloud through the main street of an ancient city in the mountains. There was remarkably little traffic, and he was saluted by every pedestrian, who stood respectfully on the side. It may be said that he and his family appreciated this. At the end it became apparent that he had driven through a pedestrian precinct. One could only have got away with that in a Rolls-Royce.

Traffic Regulations

There was no general speed limit in Jersey until the 60's, although one could be penalised for 'excessive speed', sometimes merely if a farmer-Centenier, working in his field, thought the car was going too fast. The average family car was hard put to get much above 40 to 45, and took a long time to reach it. Stopping took a long time, too. Performance cars could, of course, go much faster, given the road conditions, and the roads were uncrowded.

Recent times have shown a dramatic increase in the number of speed limits, of varying speeds. It would seem that figures hold a fascination for some people which has little regard for fact, and it is astonishingly difficult to hold down to 20 mph in an area where 30 mph is safe; many such restrictions must lead to a loss of respect for the law. The limits vary from 15 mph to 20, 30, and the all-island 40 mph. It should be far more important, albeit more difficult, to penalise dangerous driving at any speed, having regard to conditions prevailing at the time, which vary continuously. The police have the job of enforcing these limits, even if 'the law is a hass', but they do not make the law. A new development is the establishment of 'green lanes', which are small lanes primarily for the use of pedestrians, where there is some justification for the 15 mph speed limit. The propaganda that we are seeing today, opposed to the car, is as absurd as the propagandist who suggests that everything should be subservient to the car; both extremes are unreasonable.

One-way streets and pedestrian precincts were things of the future until after the War, and one could drive up and down King and Queen Streets, even parking outside premises while one went about one's affairs. Policemen on point duty wore white tunics and solar helmets in hot weather, and looked extremely smart.

We are told that road manners generally are better here than in the UK, although we have some glaring exceptions, such as treating hire car drivers very badly in too many cases. Certainly, in the commuting areas round the major urban areas in the UK, pushing and shoving are the order of the day, and it is likely that our 'filter in turn' signs would not be worth the value of the paint if they were used on British roads: they are probably unique to Jersey.

In 1962 the Police Chief reported that the road toll had been halved, compared to the previous year, but that accidents were slightly up.

Motor Tax

It is now almost fifty years since the Occupation, which made such an impact on the local motoring history; but a proper review would fill several volumes. It has been seen that most car manufacturers regarded Jersey as part of the export market immediately after the war, which did much to alleviate the severe shortage of new cars, as was the position in Britain. It was much needed, as the Island had lost so many that had been requisitioned. There did seem to be a relatively large number of big American cars from about 1930 in the early post-war days. New cars were also very much cheaper here than in Britain, as there was no punitive purchase tax on them; even today the Island purchaser of a new car is not faced with the same costs in the form of VAT and car tax.

The annual tax still varied with the horse-power, while it was changed to a flat rate in the UK to assist the export market. This change also led to better engines when the highly artificial RAC 'horse-power rating' was dropped. The tax in Jersey on a ten horse-power car in 1953 was £5. The fairly small car of one or one and a half litres engine capacity remains much the most popular in the Island, despite the dropping of the tax variable with the size of the engine: the bigger the car the more costly it is likely to be to buy and to run. The much greater efficiency of today's engines means that a small one can give a performance that would demand a vastly larger one in the older days. Today there is no annual tax on cars.

Figures suggest that the number of vehicles on the roads has reached its peak, at any rate for the present. Many households possess several cars, but there is inadequate off-road parking, and this contributes to congestion on the highway.

Car Ferries

The Ro-Ro ferry has been a comparatively new arrival, with services to the UK and St. Malo. Prior to its coming, cars had to be craned on and off the ferry, under the apprehensive eye of the owner. Disasters did not seem to happen, but one was always expecting them. The drive-on, drive-off ferries have made the turn-round times potentially much quicker and easier, and much less fraught. The latest happening is the fast Wavepiercer vessel between the Islands and the UK, owned by Commodore Shipping. Another high-speed service has now come into use for the St. Malo route by Emeraude Ferries, but this has had technical problems.

British Air Ferries flew services to and from the Mainland in the late 50's and 60's, but were unable to make them pay, and had to distcontinue. The planes could carry up to three reasonable-sized cars comfortably, and at various times used Hern or Eastleigh airports, and also Cherbourg or Dinard. It was expensive for the fare-payers, but was quick, and avoided the extras that go with the sea ferry, such as restaurant or cabin charges. One car owner recalls having a special flight laid on for him, after the scheduled service had been discontinued. His large car went on board, but the destination airport had disposed of its loading and unloading ramp; so another aircraft had to be placed door against door, the car driven across, and then flown on to Coventry to unload. The intention of the journey was to get to somewhere in the Sussex area, so there was no saving of time in this case.

The Havelat Ro-Ro unloading at Elizabeth Harbour, St. Helier. Opposite: Author's Triumph TR2 being craned onto car ferry in 1955.

Parking

Traffic Wardens made their arrival, dating from about 1962. Originally they were employed by the Parish of St. Helier, but have now been transferred to the Defence Committee, alongside the States Police, and are based in the Halkett Place sub-station. Before they came into being, uniformed men were used on point duty. relieving the police of that job. The function of the Wardens continues to be taking care of point duty, but also checking on improper parking, and generally watching the traffic situation. This relieves the Police themselves of a lot of work, and helps to avoid the often-repeated comment from illegal parkers, 'Haven't you got anything better to do?' Most of the time the Wardens are a great assistance to the responsible driver, but there is a few who are less friendly and stick to the letter of the law. One may be unable to argue about this, but it does not make for the very good relations that are enjoyed by most of the Wardens. Several parishes now employ their own traffic wardens, who do not come under the States Police.

Parking discs are required to be displayed in the car in many areas of Town and other semi-urban areas and a newer requirement in some places is a 'scratch card'. The intention of both of these is to control the parking of cars, and to show the length of time that a car has been parked; the permissible time varies from place to place. It is confusing, especially to visitors, that both systems should exist side by side. Special areas are designated for disabled drivers, and penalties may be applied for abuse of these: those marked 'Doctors Only' have no force in law, and many drivers find them convenient spots. In fact, doctors are given considerable latitude, provided they do not misuse it, and they could not carry out their duties without.

Above: The tunnel under Fort Regent which allows easy access either side of St. Helier. Opened in 1970.
Below: The underpass at the Harbour, opened 1994.

*Above: Car parking in the Weighbridge in the early 1950s.
Below: Traffic Warden overseeing yellow box opposite Library Place.*

Motor Museum

A Motor Museum was founded in St. Peter in 1973 by Mr. F M Wilcock and the late Mr. Richard Mayne. The former has long experience of vintage and veteran motoring, and the latter was a Jersey historian. Like almost all such establishments, the Museum suffers from lack of space for all its exhibits and potential exhibits. It has two main aims, firstly that of showing the Jersey scene, in pictures and artifacts, and secondly housing and displaying cars, many of which have been in Mr. Wilcock's family. Some of these he has traced and recovered from world-wide distribution after they had left his family's possession. Some items have been given to the Museum, and some are on loan. Unlike some musea, the cars are in immaculate or near-immaculate condition. Other displays include an old AA telephone box, the development of sparking plugs, and of car lights. It is open during the summer months.

Coping with Traffic Growth

Maintenance of the main roads is the responsibility of the Public Services Department, while the parishes are responsible for the minor roads within their boundaries. This means, among other things, that the Roads Committee of St. Martin has the Ecrehous in its purlieu. A broad plan was drawn up some years ago for the future development of the road system, in what is referred to as The Red Book.

In pursuit of the idea that traffic should be kept moving, many of our roads have been much improved, and Victoria Avenue has become twin-track. Other major improvements have included the tunnel between the Weighbridge and the Route de Fort in 1970. Public Works published a report in 1976, insisting that its plans must be implemented *in toto*, the alternative being chaos; these included a second tunnel, widening the Route de Fort, and a new major road system in the Bel Royal- Beaumont area. It also called for a restriction on hire purchase, purchase tax on cars over 1800cc, roadworthiness tests, parking restrictions, with increased penalties, but allowing free parking in Town for mopeds and motor cycles. It also recommended subsidies for public transport. Senator J Le Marquand was severely criticised for disagreeing.

The Island population is at present in the region of 85,000, with a car density of about 0.6 per head; this is a very high density, and is in fact a world record. It represents an opulent culture. Hire cars form a significant proportion, but are fewer than they have been – 8,000 in 1992, compared with 12,000 in 1988.

There can be no argument about the amount of traffic, and the inability of the Island's roads to carry it all. At the same time, there cannot be any serious wish to refuse a responsible adult of his reasonable right to have and to use his own private transport. Public transport is inadequate, but we are led to understand that, even if it were adequate, the public would be unwilling to give up its private transport. The very real difficulty is just where to strike the balance, a problem which is now at the heart of the debate on the future of the Motor Car in Jersey.

Other titles from SEAFLOWER BOOKS on the Channel Islands are as follows:

JERSEY RAMBLES
by John Le Dain
This book describes the routes of 28 rambles, from easy twenty-minute strolls to longer, more demanding rambles.
All aspects of the Jersey landscape are included here, from the rugged and magnificent north coast to the gentler charms of the island's well-wooded, south-sloping valleys.
128 pages; Pen & ink drawings plus 28 maps, Price £4.95

THE JERSEY LILY
by Sonia Hillsdon
Born Emilie Le Breton in Jersey in 1853, married to Edward Langtry at the age of twenty, Lillie Langtry was destined to be universally known as 'The Jersey Lily', the most beautiful woman in the world.
128 pages; fully illustrated; Price £4.95
'This book is thorough, well-written and entertaining.' – *The Jersey Society in London Bulletin.*

JERSEY: NOT QUITE BRITISH
by David Le Feuvre
This book is about an island, its history, its culture and its people. The author outlines events which helped to form the special character of the men and women who were Jersey's original inhabitants.
'This is gripping reading, colourful, proud and sad. It is not only an enlightening and entertaining work, but also an important one, whose author has done Jersey an enduring service by vividly conveying and recording the true nature of what is lost.' – *Jersey Evening Post.*
160 pages; illustrated; Price £5.95

JERSEY IN LONDON
by Brian Ahier Read
In 1895 a lone Jerseyman in London arranged a meeting with friends from Jersey who worked in the city. *Jersey in London* tells the story of how that small group of expatriates grew into a flourishing organisation. Its members have included some of the most eminent Jersey people of the century. For the Jersey historian this book offers a unique insight into a hitherto little known aspect of real Jersey folk and members of some well-known local families.
192 pages; illustrated; fully indexed; Price £6.95

JERSEY OCCUPATION DIARY

Her story of the German Occupation, 1940-45
by Nan Le Ruez

'Now a new book has been added to the list of those which speak accurately, candidly and with authority about the Occupation ... As well as painting a comprehensive picture of the daily round of drudgery which was necessary to run the farm and keep everyone fed and clothed in those most trying of times, the diary is also a record of more personal suffering ... Anyone who reads this account is likely to be impressed by its directness, its clarity and the depth of feeling it reveals ...'

from a review in the Jersey Evening Post.

304 pages; pencil drawings, photographs and map; Price £9.95

LIFE ON SARK

by Jennifer Cochrane

What is it really like to live in a small island community? Most holidaymakers to Sark are day visitors during the summer season – the impression they gain is very different to the reality of the winter months and the rest of the year.

This well informed and fondly written book is guaranteed to delight anyone intrigued by this island gem, which is perhaps the Channel Island with the greatest mystique.

128 pages; 42 black & white photographs; 12 pencil drawings; map; Price £4.95

SEAFLOWER BOOKS are published in paperback and are reasonably priced, though their design and presentation is of a high standard with good quality illustrations integrated into the text. We intend that our list will build into a body of work to represent the best writing about the real Channel Islands, in a format and at a price which will be accessible to the greatest number of readers. Comments and suggestions from readers are always welcome.

SEAFLOWER BOOKS may be obtained through local bookshops or direct from the publishers, post-free, on receipt of net price, at:

> 1 The Shambles, Bradford on Avon, Wiltshire, BA15 1JS
> Tel/ Fax 0225 863595

SEAFLOWER BOOKS is an imprint of Ex Libris Press which publishes a range of books on the themes of history, countryside, walking guides, biography and literature. Please ask for our free, illustrated list.